Bidding &
Managing
Government
Construction

Theodore J. Trauner, Jr., PE, PP

Michael H. Payne, Esq.

Bidding & Managing Government Construction

Theodore J. Trauner, Jr., PE, PP

Michael H. Payne, Esq.

R.S. MEANS COMPANY, INC.
CONSTRUCTION CONSULTANTS & PUBLISHERS
100 Construction Plaza
P.O. Box 800
Kingston, Ma 02364-0800
(617) 585-7880

The editors for this book were Mary Greene, Julia Willard, and Ernest Williams. Typesetting was supervised by Helen Marcella. The book and jacket were designed by Norman Forgit. Illustrations by Carl Linde.

Printed in the United States of America

10 9 8 7 6 5 4 3 2 1

Library of Congress Cataloging in Publication Data

ISBN 0-87629-111-6

This book is dedicated to the thousands of government employees, contractors, subcontractors, architects, and engineers, who, through their combined efforts, make the system work.

Table of Contents

Foreword

Lack of familiarity with government procedures has prevented many contractors from pursuing work with this major purchaser of construction services. This obstacle can be overcome by knowledge of government requirements and effective management strategies. This book provides the information needed to deal with every facet of government contracting, from the preparation of the bid, through change orders, disputes, and negotiations.

Chapter 1, "Bidding Government Projects," explains the procurement process. The government's bidding methods are presented, along with its guidelines for choosing contractors. Types of contracts, common problems in the bidding process, and bid protest procedures are also discussed. Chapter 2 follows up with a summary of Acts of Congress which apply to government contracting. Also included is a list of supplemental regulations for particular federal agencies.

The construction contract is the cornerstone in the relationship between the government and the contractor. The components of the contract package are described in Chapter 3, which also shows the forms that are used and highlights ten key clauses. Once the contract is formalized, it must be effectively administered in order to meet the requirements of the plans and specifications, within the budget and on schedule. Chapter 4 provides guidelines for achieving these goals.

Chapters 5 and 6 are concerned with the kinds of changes that can occur on a government construction project. These chapters present methods for determining the responsibility and the impacts of various changes, and the procedures for processing these changes. Chapter 7 goes on to explain how to estimate the cost of changes. It includes specific formulas and strategies for obtaining the most accurate costs. Chapter 8 covers the government audit process, and suggests ways in which a contractor can prepare for this procedure.

Negotiations are a key element in government contracting. With proper preparation and technique, negotiations can head off the more costly and time-consuming disputes process. Chapter 9 explains how to prepare and deal with government officials in negotiations. When disputes cannot be avoided, they should be handled as efficiently as possible, and according to government procedures. Chapters 10 and 11 outline the disputes process. Finally, Chapter 12 lists the federal agencies, describing the differences in their organizations and requirements.

Throughout the book, all references to government regulations appear in brackets as follows: [FAR 46]. FAR refers to the Federal Acquisition Regulation; U.S.C. denotes the United States Code; CFR represents the Code of Federal Regulations; and Eng BCA stands for the Engineering Board of Contract Appeals. Other abbreviations are identified on the "Abbreviations" page at the back of the book.

Although this book has been written with the federal government as its focus, the principles and procedures discussed are generally applicable to state and city government construction projects as well.

The Editors

Acknowledgments

The authors would like to acknowledge the following individuals for their capable assistance: Timothy A. Sullivan, Esquire, whose legal research was invaluable; and Gerrie M. Keane and Lizanne Cotton, who spent countless hours typing, editing, assembling materials, and coordinating our efforts.

Introduction

In recent years, construction firms have witnessed tremendous competition for government contracts and have encountered increasing difficulty in dealing with federal agencies during contract administration. Due to the level of competition for this work, contractors must ensure that both the government and their competitors comply with the myriad rules and regulations governing the bidding and negotiation process to protect their competitive position in the market. Moreover, problems encountered during performance, which in the past were amicably resolved at the field level, are now frequently reviewed in an overly defensive and negative manner by government representatives. As a result, the number of construction contract protests, claims, and appeals is at an all-time high. To survive and prosper in this environment, contractors must be familiar with their rights and responsibilities in contracting with the government.

Recognizing this need, this book is designed as a practical guide to contracting with the government. Addressing the process from bidding to close-out, the book endeavors to simplify and condense the maze of government rules and regulations so that both seasoned and inexperienced contractors alike can successfully conduct business with the government. The reader will, therefore, gain a thorough knowledge of the regulatory framework within which all parties to a government contract must operate. Moreover, because this book adopts a practical rather than theoretical or esoteric approach, it provides proven techniques for exercising contractor's rights and meeting their responsibilities in the arena of government contracting.

In order to efficiently and profitably contract with the government, contractors, subcontractors, designers, and attorneys involved in government construction should:

- Have a working knowledge of the typically complex and disjointed federal contracting requirements.
- Understand the government's philosophy of construction contracts.
- Be aware of how to protect one's interests when performing work under a federal government contract.

- Thoroughly understand all phases of the administration of a government construction contract.
- Understand what goes on "behind the scenes" as the government administers the construction contract.

These concepts are explained in this book to provide the basic framework for understanding the government construction process. Contractors, subcontractors, designers, and attorneys are all involved with government construction projects and, therefore, may benefit from this information. This book may also benefit the many government employees who implement the controlling regulations and seek to administer construction contracts more efficiently.

Chapter One
Bidding Government Construction Projects

Chapter One

Bidding Government Construction Projects

To successfully contract with the government, a contractor must not only have a good working knowledge of construction practices and procedures, but must also be thoroughly aware of appropriate government regulations. Government agencies are free to acquire supplies and services only according to the statutes enacted by Congress. Clearly, the contractor who is well versed in the workings of government procurement and administrative procedures will have the advantage. This knowledge begins with the bidding process. Procedures for bidding government projects are discussed in this chapter. Included are acquisition methods, contract types and forms, mistakes in bidding, and bid protest procedures.

Acquisition Methods

Every government project begins with the identification of a need for supplies or services. A construction project may be a new facility or may be the result of an ongoing operational program to maintain or improve an existing facility. Next, the project must be funded. The budget for a project may be specified in a specific line item in the federal budget, or may be part of the budget for an existing facility. Once the need has been identified and funded, it is the responsibility of the government agency to prepare a set of plans and specifications and to determine the method by which a construction contractor will be solicited.

The preparation of plans and specifications is a key element in a government construction project. The government creates an estimate based on these plans and specifications, and determines whether the available funding is sufficient to meet the requirements of the project. The government's choice of acquisition method is based, in large part, on the nature and clarity of the plans and specifications.

In the past, government plans and specifications were usually prepared by government personnel. Today, it is common practice for the government to secure outside architectural/engineering services. This practice has resulted in a reduction of in-house expertise on the part of the federal agencies, and has placed a greater burden on the architectural/engineering firms which must ensure that the plans and specifications are adequate for purposes of the federal solicitation.

The Competition in Contracting Act of 1984 [41 U.S.C. 253] resulted in a change in some of the acquisition terminology in government contracts (see Chapter 2, "Laws and Regulations"). For example, the term for the most common type of acquisition method, *formal advertising*, was changed to *sealed bidding*; the term for the second major acquisition method (formerly negotiated procurement) was changed to *competitive proposal*. The basic requirements of these acquisition methods are, however, unchanged. Sealed bidding remains the primary method by which the federal government procures construction contract services.

Sealed Bidding

Sealed bidding involves competitive bids, public opening of bids, and awards. [FAR 14] Although the sealed bidding method places the greatest risk on the contractor, it also presents the greatest opportunity for reward. The elements of sealed bidding, as defined by federal regulations, are outlined in Figure 1.1.

When using the sealed bidding method, it is extremely important that the plans and specifications clearly and accurately describe the government's needs. It is the government's intention to secure competition on the basis of *price*. Each bidder must, therefore, have the same understanding of what is required so that each is bidding on the same basic quantities of required materials and labor. The competition is based on price alone, with each bidder competing to provide precisely the same construction services or product, but each offering to do it at a different price. Unfortunately, when plans and specifications are not adequate, bidders are often misled and prices may become distorted through misinterpretation of the plans and specifications. Ironically, under these conditions, the bidder who really understands the plans and specifications, and who may be the most qualified to perform the work, may bid at a higher price than those who are less competent or knowledgeable.

Responsiveness and Responsibility

Award of the contract under sealed bidding practices is made to the bidder who is determined *responsible* and who submits the lowest bid deemed *responsive*. If a bidder is not the apparent low bidder at the time of bid opening, an evaluation of responsiveness and responsibility is not made.

The *responsiveness of the bid* is determined at the time of the bid opening. In order to be found responsive, "a bid must comply in all material respects with the invitation for bids." [FAR 14.301] This means that the bidder must be willing to comply with all of the essential requirements of the solicitation. If a bidder takes exception in the bid to any of the essential requirements, the bid may be rejected as nonresponsive and awarded to the next lowest bidder who is both responsive and responsible.

A bid is also examined to determine whether or not it conforms to the essential requirements of the invitation. Areas of nonresponsiveness may involve issues of price, quantity, quality, or performance time. If a bidder takes exception to the requirements for any of these four elements, the bid will most assuredly be rejected as nonresponsive. For example, if the government specifies that a project is to be completed within 300 days and a bidder submits a bid indicating that the project will be completed in 301 days, the bidder has deviated from an essential requirement of the solicitation and the bid will be rejected as nonresponsive. Similarly, a bidder who fails to bid on all of the required line items on the bidding schedule or who deviates from the quantitative or qualitative requirements of the solicitation is risking rejection without any further opportunity to change this aspect of his bid.

A nonresponsive bid may not be corrected after bid opening in order to make it responsive. To do so would enable a bidder to have "two bites at the apple" and would degrade the integrity of the competitive bidding system. Therefore, corrections to

The Elements of Sealed Bidding

- *Preparation of Invitation for Bids*: The invitation must describe the requirements of the government construction project clearly, accurately, and completely. Unnecessarily restrictive specifications or requirements that might unduly limit the number of bidders are prohibited. The invitation must include all documents (whether attached or incorporated by reference) required by prospective bidders for the purpose of bidding.
- *Publicizing the Invitation for Bids*: The invitation must be publicized through distribution to prospective bidders, posting in public places, and such other means as may be appropriate. Publicizing must occur a sufficient time before public opening of bids to enable prospective bidders to prepare and submit bids.
- *Submission of Bids*: Bidders must submit sealed bids to be opened at the time and place stated in the solicitation for the public opening of bids.
- *Evaluation of Bids*: Bids are evaluated without discussions.
- *Contract Award*: After bids are opened publicly, an award is made with reasonable promptness to the responsible bidder whose bid conforms to the invitation for bids and is the most advantageous to the government. The award is based only on the price and the price-related factors included in the invitation. [FAR 14.101]

Figure 1.1

nonresponsive bids are not allowed, even though it may be to the government's financial advantage to allow such correction in order to retain the lowest possible price.

A *responsible contractor* is one who demonstrates the capability to perform all of the contract requirements. To be found responsible, a bidder must have the following resources, skills, and qualifications:

- Adequate financial resources to perform the contract or the ability to obtain them.
- The ability to comply with the required or proposed delivery or performance schedule, taking into consideration all existing commercial and government business commitments.
- A satisfactory performance record (i.e., satisfactory ratings on previous contracts based on certain criteria, including timely performance, quality of workmanship, efficiency of management, and adherence to rules and regulations).
- A satisfactory record of integrity and business ethics (i.e., a record free of prior default terminations or allegations of fraud, false claims, or false statements to government agencies).
- The necessary organization, experience, accounting and operational control, and technical skills, or the ability to obtain them (including, as appropriate, such elements as production control procedures, property control systems, and quality assurance measures applicable to materials to be produced or services to be performed by the prospective contractor and subcontractors).
- The necessary production, construction, and technical equipment and facilities, or the ability to obtain them.
- Any other qualifications for eligibility to receive an award under applicable laws and regulations. [FAR 9.104]

Unlike responsiveness, which must be determined at the time of the bid opening, *responsibility* can be demonstrated at any time prior to award. Therefore, a contractor initially found to be nonresponsible can discuss the matter with the contracting officer and make changes in order to demonstrate his responsibility.

The government determines a bidder's responsibility by performing a *pre-award survey*. The depth of this survey is very much dependent upon the agency's familiarity with the particular bidder. If this is a company's first government contract or first experience with a particular agency or installation, a bidder should anticipate a detailed pre-award survey commensurate with the size and complexity of the project. If the pre-award survey determines that the bidder is nonresponsible and the bidder is unable to convince the contracting officer that steps can be taken to correct any detected deficiencies, the bid will be rejected and the award will be made to the next lowest bidder who is both responsive and responsible.

Certificate of Competency (COC)

A small business which is found to be nonresponsible has the opportunity to overturn the contracting officer's finding of nonresponsibility through the Small Business Administration (SBA). Within fifteen days after receiving notice that a small business lacks certain elements of responsibility, the SBA will inform the small business of the contracting officer's determination. The SBA will offer the small business the opportunity to apply for a Certificate of Competency (COC). Upon receipt of a timely application and the required supporting documentation, the SBA then sends its own investigator, or team of investigators, to visit the small business in order to investigate the elements of responsibility which the agency found lacking. The SBA has fifteen days to decide whether to issue a Certificate of Competency. If the SBA disagrees with the agency's finding, it will issue a Certificate of Competency which overcomes the finding of nonresponsibility by the contracting officer and makes it possible for the bidder to receive the award.

The Certificate of Competency (COC) procedure is an excellent vehicle by which small businesses can obtain a fair review of the responsibility determinations of federal agencies. The SBA is not hesitant to disagree with the findings of the agency and usually makes every effort to give the small business the opportunity to demonstrate its responsibility. Although agencies usually abide by the determination of the SBA, if the contracting officer disagrees with the SBA's issuance of a COC, the matter can be referred to the SBA Central Office for purposes of a final ruling. [FAR 19.602] Unfortunately, there is no similar COC procedure available to a large business that is evaluated as nonresponsible.

Competitive Proposals

The second major acquisition method used by the government is competitive proposals. Through the use of the competitive proposal solicitation form, the government solicits offers from prospective contractors. When the offers are received, the procedure permits bargaining and usually affords an opportunity for contractors to revise their offers before the award of the contract. The negotiating involves altering initial assumptions and positions regarding the price, schedule, technical requirements, type of contract, or other terms of the proposed contract through discussion and persuasion. [FAR 15.102]

Although sealed bidding is the acquisition method most frequently used by the federal government to procure construction services, use of the competitive proposal method is on the rise. Unlike sealed bidding, where price is determined at the time of bid opening, the competitive proposal method may provide an opportunity for a bidder to change its price prior to award (assuming that the government opens up negotiations and does not exercise its right to award the contract on the basis of initial offers).

When negotiations are opened, the government determines which offers are within the competitive range. The *competitive range* is established by evaluating which offers are most likely to result in the ultimate award of the contract. Frequently, the offer that is closest to the government's estimate or most consistent with the evaluation criteria applied by the government will be classified as within the competitive range. Negotiations will be limited to the contractors who submitted those offers. Each contractor is then invited to discuss the proposal with the government negotiator and is given the opportunity to ask questions and ultimately to make changes in the original offer. It is not legal, however, for the government negotiator to conduct an auction or to advise contractors of the position of other contractors' offers.

When negotiations are completed, the government allows the contractors to submit a best and final offer. Award is then made to the contractor who best meets the evaluation criteria listed in the solicitation. Unlike sealed bidding, which limits competition to price, the evaluation criteria for competitive proposals may include matters other than price, such as:

- Technical capacity
- Management staff
- Experience
- Quality control
- Proposed performance schedule
- Proposed project staffing (superintendents, quality control, project manager)
- Design (such as design and building projects for family housing)

Unlike sealed bids, which must be awarded on a firm fixed-price basis, a negotiated procurement may be awarded on either a firm fixed-price or cost-reimbursement type of contract.

Types of Contracts

The government uses a number of different types of contracts in order to provide the flexibility necessary to accommodate the large variety and volume of supplies and services required by federal agencies. The contract types vary according to (1) the degree and timing of the responsibility assumed by the contractor for the cost of performance and (2) the amount and nature of the profit incentive offered to the contractor for achieving or exceeding the specified standards or goals. [FAR 16.101]

The two most frequently used contracts are:

- Fixed-price contracts [FAR 16.2]
- Cost reimbursement contracts [FAR 16.3]

A fixed-price contract does not allow adjustment of the contract price based on the costs incurred by the contractor during performance. A cost-reimbursement contract provides for payment of allowable incurred costs during performance.

Within the fixed-price contract category is the firm fixed-price contract, in which the contractor has full responsibility for the performance costs and resulting profit (or loss). On the other end is the cost-plus-fixed-fee contract, a type of cost reimbursement contract in which the contractor has minimal responsibility for the performance costs, and the negotiated fee (profit) is fixed.

Fixed-Price Contracts

The fixed price contract is the most basic and widely used type of formally advertised government contract, whereby the contractor agrees to furnish to the government the supplies or services called for at the bid price. A firm fixed-price contract is awarded at the sealed bid price. That price is not adjusted — upward or downward — by the costs incurred by the contractor during performance. All contracts resulting from sealed bids are awarded on a firm fixed-price basis (or firm fixed-price with economic price adjustment). The firm fixed-price contract "best utilizes the basic profit motive of business enterprise," and should be used when the risk involved is "minimal or can be predicted with an acceptable degree of certainty." [FAR 16.103(b)]

To determine whether the firm fixed-price contract method is suitable for a particular project, the contracting officer must do the following. First, he must discover that the supplies or services are being procured on the basis of reasonably definite functional or detailed specifications. The contracting officer must also see that the qualifications are being met. Conditions for the firm fixed price contract are summarized in Figure 1.2.

Cost-Reimbursement Contracts

Cost-reimbursement contracts provide for payment of allowable incurred costs to the extent prescribed in the contract. Cost-reimbursement contracts establish an estimate of the total costs. The purpose is to obligate funds and establish a ceiling that the contracting company may not exceed, except at its own risk, without the approval of the contracting officer. [FAR 16.301-1] Most importantly, "cost-reimbursement contracts are suitable for use only when uncertainties involved in contract performance do not permit costs to be estimated with sufficient

Conditions for the Firm Fixed-Price Contract

- Adequate price competition.
- Reasonable price comparisons with prior purchases of the same or similar supplies or services made on a competitive basis or supported by valid cost or pricing data.
- Available cost or pricing information, which permits realistic estimates of the probable cost of performance.
- Identifiable performance uncertainties, the cost impact of which can be reasonably estimated. The contractor must be willing to accept a firm fixed price, representing an assumption of the risk involved. [FAR 16.202-2]

Figure 1.2

accuracy to use any type of fixed-price contract." [FAR 16.301-2] A cost-reimbursement contract may only be used under the conditions shown in Figure 1.3.

Cost-Plus-Fixed-Fee

A cost-plus-fixed-fee contract is a type of cost-reimbursement contract. This arrangement provides for the payment to the contractor of a negotiated fee that is determined prior to signing the contract. The cost-plus-fixed-fee contract is virtually the only cost-reimbursement type contract that has been used in government construction contracting. The fixed fee does not vary with actual cost, but may be adjusted as a result of changes in the work to be performed under the contract. A cost-plus-fixed-fee contract permits contracting for projects that might otherwise present too great a risk to contractors. On the other hand, it provides the contractor with only a minimum incentive to control costs. [FAR 16.306]

Other Types of Cost-Reimbursement Contracts

Other types of cost-reimbursement contracts include cost-sharing contracts, cost-plus-incentive-fee contracts, and cost-plus-award-fee contracts, all of which are generally not found in construction contracts. The contract forms outlined below are for cost-reimbursement.

There are also various incentive contracts, such as award-plus-incentive-fee and award-plus-target-fee, which differ from both fixed price and cost reimbursement contracts. [FAR 16.4]

Form of Contract

Solicitation/Contract Form

The Standard Form 33, Solicitation Offer and Award (SF 33), is included in the sealed bid form and submitted by bidders at the time of bid opening. This form is shown in Figure 1.4. A construction contractor is required to execute this standardized contract document in order to perform construction work for the

---

Conditions for the Cost Reimbursement Contract

- The contractor's accounting system is adequate for determining costs applicable to the contract.
- Appropriate government surveillance during performance will provide reasonable assurance that efficient methods and effective cost controls are used.
- A determination and findings have been executed, in accordance with agency procedures, showing that (1) this contract type is likely to be less costly than any other type or (2) it is impractical to obtain supplies or services of a kind or quality required without the use of this contract type. [FAR 16.301-3]

Figure 1.3

government. The government then completes the "Award" section of the solicitation for the successful bidder (the lowest responsive, responsible bidder). It is very important for the bidder to understand that government contract forms and documents must be accepted without changing a single word.

Uniform Contract Format

The contract has a number of parts, many of which contain standardized language. A contractor can expect the format to include sections with the standard Federal Acquisition Regulation (FAR) contract clauses; special and technical contract requirements tailored to the specific project; sections on quality control, submittals, and environmental requirements; and various attachments, including the amendments, specifications, and drawings. Generally, the solicitation and resulting contract are organized as shown in Figure 1.5. [FAR 14.201-1]

Terms of the Contract

The bidder should read the entire contract prior to submitting a bid and should pay particular attention to Section H, "Special Contract Requirements," and Section L, "Instructions to Bidders." The bidder should also note under Section I, "Contract Clauses," whether the government included the full text of the clauses. If the government incorporated the clauses by a reference index, the bidder should obtain the full text of the clauses in order to become familiar with all of the rights and obligations in the contract.

The contractor should also review the contract upon receipt and before execution to ensure that all of the documents noted on the SF 33 are included and that the government has not included different specifications, drawings, or special terms which were not presented with the solicitation.

The Bidding Process

In government construction contracting, often the most difficult task for the contractor is trying to bid the project in such a way that being the low bidder will still earn the company a profit. Attaining this goal requires a thorough understanding of the rules of the bidding process. The contractor must also be aware of some problem areas that are commonly associated with bidding. An awareness of these issues may help to prevent bid rejection or denial of additional compensation for extra or different work. The following paragraphs offer some guidelines for individual elements of the bidding process.

Errors and Omissions in Plans and Specifications

One of the most significant problem areas in bidding involves the errors and omissions that may exist in government plans and specifications. A contractor who recognizes a deficiency in the plans and specifications (which are a part of the solicitation) is required to bring that deficiency to the government's attention. Failure to do so may result in the rejection of a later claim for the following reason. Failure to alert government representatives to an obvious or known defect denies them the opportunity to correct their solicitation and, consequently, to place all bidders on an equal footing. It is highly risky for any

SOLICITATION, OFFER AND AWARD

SOLICITATION, OFFER AND AWARD	**1. THIS CONTRACT IS A RATED ORDER UNDER DPAS (15 CFR 350)** ▶ **RATING** **PAGE OF PAGES**

2. CONTRACT NO.	3. SOLICITATION NO.	4. TYPE OF SOLICITATION	5. DATE ISSUED	6. REQUISITION/PURCHASE NO.
		☐ SEALED BID (IFB) ☐ NEGOTIATED (RFP)		

7. ISSUED BY CODE [ ]   **8. ADDRESS OFFER TO** *(If other than Item 7)*

NOTE: In sealed bid solicitations "offer" and "offeror" mean "bid" and "bidder".

SOLICITATION

9. Sealed offers in original and _____ copies for furnishing the supplies or services in the Schedule will be received at the place specified in Item 8, or if handcarried, in the depository located in _____ until _____ local time _____
(Hour)   (Date)

CAUTION — LATE Submissions, Modifications, and Withdrawals: See Section L, Provision No. 52.214-7 or 52.215-10. All offers are subject to all terms and conditions contained in this solicitation.

10. FOR INFORMATION CALL: ▶ A. NAME | B. TELEPHONE NO. *(Include area code)* *(NO COLLECT CALLS)*

11. TABLE OF CONTENTS

(√)	SEC.	DESCRIPTION	PAGE(S)	(√)	SEC.	DESCRIPTION	PAGE(S)
		PART I — THE SCHEDULE				**PART II — CONTRACT CLAUSES**	
	A	SOLICITATION/CONTRACT FORM			I	CONTRACT CLAUSES	
	B	SUPPLIES OR SERVICES AND PRICES/COSTS				**PART III — LIST OF DOCUMENTS, EXHIBITS AND OTHER ATTACH.**	
	C	DESCRIPTION/SPECS./WORK STATEMENT			J	LIST OF ATTACHMENTS	
	D	PACKAGING AND MARKING				**PART IV — REPRESENTATIONS AND INSTRUCTIONS**	
	E	INSPECTION AND ACCEPTANCE			K	REPRESENTATIONS, CERTIFICATIONS AND OTHER STATEMENTS OF OFFERORS	
	F	DELIVERIES OR PERFORMANCE					
	G	CONTRACT ADMINISTRATION DATA			L	INSTRS., CONDS., AND NOTICES TO OFFERORS	
	H	SPECIAL CONTRACT REQUIREMENTS			M	EVALUATION FACTORS FOR AWARD	

OFFER *(Must be fully completed by offeror)*

NOTE: Item 12 does not apply if the solicitation includes the provisions at 52.214-16, Minimum Bid Acceptance Period.

12. In compliance with the above, the undersigned agrees, if this offer is accepted within _____ calendar days *(60 calendar days unless a different period is inserted by the offeror)* from the date for receipt of offers specified above, to furnish any or all items upon which prices are offered at the price set opposite each item, delivered at the designated point(s), within the time specified in the schedule.

13. DISCOUNT FOR PROMPT PAYMENT *(See Section I, Clause No. 52-232-8)* ▶	10 CALENDAR DAYS %	20 CALENDAR DAYS %	30 CALENDAR DAYS %	CALENDAR DAYS %

14. ACKNOWLEDGMENT OF AMENDMENTS *(The offeror acknowledges receipt of amendments to the SOLICITATION for offerors and related documents numbered and dated:)*	AMENDMENT NO.	DATE	AMENDMENT NO.	DATE

15A. NAME AND ADDRESS OF OFFEROR	CODE [ ] FACILITY [ ]	16. NAME AND TITLE OF PERSON AUTHORIZED TO SIGN OFFER *(Type or print)*

15B. TELEPHONE NO. *(Include area code)*	15C. CHECK IF REMITTANCE ADDRESS IS DIFFERENT FROM ABOVE - ENTER SUCH ADDRESS IN SCHEDULE. ☐	17. SIGNATURE	18. OFFER DATE

AWARD *(To be completed by Government)*

19. ACCEPTED AS TO ITEMS NUMBERED	20. AMOUNT	21. ACCOUNTING AND APPROPRIATION

22. AUTHORITY FOR USING OTHER THAN FULL AND OPEN COMPETITION:

☐ 10 U.S.C. 2304(c)( )   ☐ 41 U.S.C. 253(c)( ) | 23. SUBMIT INVOICES TO ADDRESS SHOWN IN ▶ ITEM *(4 copies unless otherwise specified)*

24. ADMINISTERED BY *(If other than Item 7)* CODE [ ]	25. PAYMENT WILL BE MADE BY CODE [ ]

26. NAME OF CONTRACTING OFFICER *(Type or print)*	27. UNITED STATES OF AMERICA *(Signature of Contracting Officer)*	28. AWARD DATE

IMPORTANT — Award will be made on this Form, or on Standard Form 26, or by other authorized official written notice.

NSN 7540-01-152-8064
PREVIOUS EDITION NOT USABLE
33-133
STANDARD FORM 33 (REV. 4-85)
Prescribed by GSA
FAR (48 CFR) 53.214(c)
☆U.S. Government Printing Office: 1985/477-063/39130

Figure 1.4

contractor to withhold information about an error or omission, with the idea of profiting from the change order when the deficiency is made known to the government during project construction.

There are times when the government does not respond in a helpful way to a bidder's notification of a possible error or omission. All too often, the response of government technical representatives is, "Bid it as you see it." This response is not at all helpful and causes the bidder to guess about the government's intentions. A contractor in this situation should either (1) protest the government's refusal to clarify the solicitation prior to bid opening or (2) notify the government of how the specification is interpreted in terms of its effect on the bid, and request notification from the government prior to bid opening as to the correctness of its interpretation of the plans and specifications.

Ambiguous Plans and Specifications
Ambiguous plans and specifications are another area fraught with the potential for later claims and appeals. A provision is

Uniform Contract Format

Section	Title
Part I	The Schedule
A	Solicitation/Contract Form
B	Supplies or Services and Prices
C	Description/Specifications
D	Packaging and Marking
E	Inspection and Acceptance
F	Deliveries for Performance
G	Contract Administration Data
H	Special Contract Requirements
Part II	Contract Clauses
I	Contract Clauses
Part III	List of Documents, Exhibits, and Other Attachments
J	List of Documents, Exhibits, and Other Attachments
Part IV	Representations and Instructions
K	Representations, Certifications, and Other Statements of Bidders
L	Instructions, Conditions, and Notices to Bidders
M	Evaluation Factors for Award

Figure 1.5

ambiguous if it is capable of having two or more meanings. If aware of such an ambiguity, the contractor is required to bring it to the government's attention prior to bidding. The consequence of failing to notify the government of an ambiguity may be the same as for failing to raise an obvious error or omission prior to bid opening. The key issue is often whether the ambiguity was truly obvious (patent) or whether it was hidden or unknown (latent). If the ambiguity is determined to be latent, the contractor would be excused from failure to raise the issue at the time of bidding. The answer varies, of course, with the facts of each particular case. It is, however, often helpful to remind government procurement officials that what appears obvious during construction, when great scrutiny is being directed to that part of the plans and specifications at issue, often goes unnoticed during the short time frame available during the bidding period.

The contractor faced with an ambiguity that could not have been anticipated at the time of bidding is entitled to an equitable adjustment of the contract for any additional costs incurred as a result of the ambiguity. Thus, if the government insists on interpreting an ambiguous specification in a way different from the bidder's interpretation, the government is liable for the extra costs. In this situation, the contractor need only demonstrate that the interpretation of the specification used at the time of bidding was reasonable (i.e., logical). It need not be the "best" interpretation, the least expensive interpretation, or the interpretation favored by the government; it need only be reasonable.

Defective Specifications

Defective specifications include those that contain either errors/omissions or ambiguities. Defective specifications are often the result of hurried or careless drafting of technical provisions and plans. Deadline pressures often result in a heavy reliance on manufacturer's literature or a company's proprietary specifications in preparing technical specifications. Problems arise when these proprietary specifications are not identified as such in the resulting plans and specifications, and the bidder is led to believe that an off-the-shelf item is readily available or that the need for the item can be met by a number of manufacturers. A tremendous burden is thereby placed on the bidder who must determine whether or not the specifications require detailed pricing during the estimating process in order to alleviate the risk that a far more expensive, proprietary item will actually be required. Bidders who suspect the hidden use of proprietary specifications should notify the government representatives prior to bidding. If necessary, they should protest the unduly restrictive nature of such solicitations. Such restrictions unquestionably increase the cost to the government.

The Bid Form and Bid Bond

Once the plans and specifications have been thoroughly evaluated and the pre-bid estimate prepared, bidders must be careful to transfer all of the information to the required bid form in the proper manner. Any deviation from the requirements of the solicitation, or failure to supply specified information or to fill in line items on the bid schedule, may result in rejection of the bid as nonresponsive. The bid must be properly signed and dated and, if required, must include a properly executed bid bond with the power of attorney on behalf of the bidder's surety. There is perhaps no part of the bid form with more potential for irregularity than the bid bond.

Proper execution of the bid bond means that all of the required information is inserted on the face of the bond so that it is clear that the bid bond applies to the solicitation involved. For example, the signature of the authorized representative of the construction firm is required on the face of the bond; and the signature of the attorney-in-fact for the bonding company is required in the appropriate block and must match the attached power of attorney. It is also important that the bonding company insert its correct liability limit in the lower right-hand corner of the bid bond form. (This liability limit is found in Treasury Circular No. 570 and is revised yearly.) Failure to either insert the proper liability limit or to have the bid bond executed by an attorney-in-fact for the bonding company (who has authority to issue a bond in the amount required for the solicitation) may result in rejection of the bid as nonresponsive.

Sophisticated bidders have long known that it is to their advantage to review the bid bond of the low bidder. In this way, they can determine whether one of the common errors has taken place which may result in the rejection of the bid and award of the contract to the next lowest bidder.

Acknowledgment of Amendments
Once the bid is prepared and includes all required information and the supporting bid bond, the bidder should make sure that all of the amendments to the solicitation have been acknowledged. Failure to acknowledge an amendment that deals with price, quantity, quality, or performance time may result in rejection of the bid as nonresponsive. For example, an amendment to the solicitation may change the technical requirements in terms of the quantity of an item or the quality of materials. The contractor's failure to acknowledge that amendment prevents the government from knowing whether the bidder intends to furnish the item as described in the original solicitation or as revised in the amendment. Since responsiveness is determined at the time of bid opening, it is not possible for the bidder to furnish an explanation *after* bid opening, and the bid will be rejected as nonresponsive. On the other hand, if the amendment changed a relatively minor item, such as the bid room number, the contracting officer may waive the failure to acknowledge the amendment as a minor informality, because it did not deal with price, quantity, quality, or performance time.

Late Bids
It is extremely important for a bidder to deliver the bid or offer at the appointed place and *on time*. Late bids or offers must be rejected and returned unopened by the contracting officer. While exceptions have been granted in cases where the bidder is able

to demonstrate government mishandling, most late bids are ultimately rejected because of the difficulty of proving government mishandling.

Mistakes in Bid Procedure

The Federal Acquisition Regulation (FAR) requires that, after the opening of bids, the contracting officer examine all bids for possible mistakes (see Chapter 2, "Laws and Regulations"). In federal government construction contracting, the procedures for dealing with mistakes in bids are far more lenient than those found in most state and local jurisdictions. This does not mean that it is easy to obtain relief for a mistake in bid, but federal procedures do allow for withdrawal, and even upward correction in certain circumstances, if the required criteria are met.

Apparent Mistakes

If there is reason to believe that a mistake has been made, the contracting officer is required to request verification of the bid, calling attention to the suspected mistake. If the mistake is clerical in nature and apparent on the face of the bid, it may be corrected by the contracting officer prior to award. Examples of apparent (obvious) mistakes are listed below.

- Misplacement of a decimal point
- Incorrect discounts (for example, 1 percent 10 days, 2 percent 20 days, 5 percent 30 days)
- Reversal of the price — free on board (f.o.b.) — destination, and price f.o.b. origin
- Mistake in designation of unit

Withdrawal of a Bid

The procedures dealing with mistakes in bids only apply to those situations where a mistake can be proven through examination of the bid and underlying bid papers. These procedures do not grant relief in the case of an error in judgment. If the bidder requests permission to withdraw a bid because of an alleged mistake, the evidence must be clear and convincing as to the existence of the mistake. When evidence is presented supporting the mistake and showing how it was made, most agencies will allow a bidder to withdraw. It is not the intention of federal agencies to enter into contracts with bidders who have indicated that they have made a mistake and who, if awarded the contract, will lose money on the project. On the contrary, federal agencies see this situation as "buying trouble" and will generally be reasonable in allowing withdrawal. A bidder must be careful, however, not to abuse this privilege.

Correction of a Mistake

The federal system allows upward correction of a bid if the low bidder is responsive to the invitation. In this case, the bidder must demonstrate, through clear and convincing evidence, both the existence of the mistake and the bid actually intended. Such a correction will not be allowed *unless* the mistake and the intended bid can be ascertained from the bid and supporting documentation. [FAR 14.406-3] Generally, as a requested upward correction becomes closer to the next lowest bid, it will be scrutinized more closely by the agency.

Another instance in which correction of a bid mistake may be requested after the award of a contract is when correction of the mistake would be favorable to the government, without changing the essential requirements of the specifications. In this situation, a modification to the contract is issued or the contract is reformed.

In some cases, the government may decide to rescind the contract through termination in view of the mistake. In all cases of alleged mistakes, however, the contractor is required to submit a written statement and documentary evidence regarding preparation of the bid, the original bid worksheets and supporting data, subcontractors' and suppliers' quotations, and any other evidence that will serve to establish the mistake. [FAR 14.406-4]

Bid Protest Procedures

A bidder who is dissatisfied with the nature or propriety of a solicitation may file a protest to the agency involved, the General Accounting Office (GAO), or the United States Claims Court. Because it is very difficult to win a protest, it is important that the bidder be certain that the matter raised is not frivolous, and that prior decisions of the United States Claims Court or the GAO have not already established the government's position on the matter. Great deference is given to the judgment of contracting officers in determining both the method of procurement and the needs of the government. Only a protest where the bidder can show that the government has violated the regulations, unduly restricted competition, or abused its discretion has any likelihood of success.

In most cases, the procedures for filing a protest directly to a federal agency are very similar to the bid protest regulations of the GAO [4 CFR Part 21]. Under these regulations an "interested party," meaning one who has an actual or prospective economic interest in the solicitation, may file a protest based on alleged improprieties in the solicitation. The protest must, however, be filed prior to bid opening (sealed bidding) or before the closing date for receipt of initial proposals (competitive proposals). In other cases, protests must be filed no later than ten working days after the basis of the protest is known or should have been known, whichever is earlier.

The protest must be in writing. If it is filed with the GAO, the protest should be addressed as follows.

General Counsel
General Accounting Office
Washington, D.C. 20548
ATTENTION: Procurement Law Control Group

The protest should include the information listed in Figure 1.6.

The bidder should furnish a copy of the protest, including the relevant documents, to the individual or location designated by the contracting agency in the solicitation for receipt of protests. It is important that the contractor protesting a solicitation procedure be prepared to address the agency's position after its administrative report is filed. Whether the matter is before the agency or the GAO, a contractor should request a conference to discuss the merits of the protest. If insufficient information has been submitted by the contractor or if the protest falls within the category of protests not in the general jurisdiction of the GAO, there is considerable risk that the protest will be dismissed summarily. The types of protests that may be dismissed without consideration of its merits are listed in Figure 1.7.

If the protest is filed with the GAO, the Competition in Contracting Act requires that a decision be issued within 90 days of the date the protest was filed (see Chapter 2, "*Laws and Regulations*"). In those cases where both parties agree to an expedited procedure, known as the *express option*, a decision is made within 45 days. While the protest is pending, the agency is prohibited from awarding a contract unless performance of the contract is in the government's best interest, or urgent and compelling circumstances significantly affecting the interests of the United States will not permit waiting for the GAO decision. If the initial protest is filed with the contracting agency, an adverse decision by the agency may subsequently be protested to the GAO within ten days of formal notification or actual or constructive knowledge of the agency decision. Bidders may also appeal the decisions of the GAO to the United States Claims Court. Generally, it is not advisable to bypass the agency or the GAO, which are the most familiar with the procurement regulations involved, in favor of approaching the Claims Court. However, a matter involving a strictly *legal interpretation* of a law or regulation should be submitted to the Claims Court.

It is also possible to file a protest *after* award of the contract, provided that the protest is filed within ten working days of the date when the basis for the protest was known or should have been known. In such cases, the notice to proceed generally will not be issued until the protest is decided, barring national urgency. If the project is already under way when the protest is

---

Information to Include in a Protest
- The name, address, and telephone number of the protester.
- An original signed by the protester or a representative, and at least one copy.
- The identity of the agency issuing the solicitation and/or the contract number.
- A detailed statement of the legal and factual grounds of the protest, including copies of relevant documents.
- A specific request for a ruling by the Comptroller General of the United States.
- The form of relief requested.

Figure 1.6

filed, work will continue and it is unlikely that termination of the contract will be ordered even if the protest is won. The federal government, in such cases, may have its "hand slapped" by the GAO, but it generally will not be forced to suffer the severe financial consequences that would result from termination of the contract after the commencement of the project.

A contractor who is successful in the protest, but is not granted award of the contract, may be entitled to bid preparation costs and attorneys' fees. However, a contractor is not permitted to recover anticipated profits, or profits lost from other projects.

Protests That May Be Dismissed Without Consideration of Merits

- Contract Administration.
- Small Business Size Standards and Standard Industrial Classification.
- The Small Business Certificate of Competency Program.
- Procurements under Section 8(a) of the Small Business Act.
- Affirmative determinations of responsibility by the contracting officer.
- Protests not filed to the GAO or the contracting agency within the applicable time limits.
- Procurement by agencies other than federal agencies as defined by Section 3 of the Federal Property and Administrative Services Act of 1949, 40 U.S.C. 472 (e.g., U.S. Postal Service, Federal Deposit Insurance Corporation, non-appropriated fund activities).
- Walsh-Healey Public Contracts Act.
- Subcontractor protests.
- Judicial proceeding.

Figure 1.7

Chapter Two
Laws and Regulations

Chapter Two
Laws and Regulations

Government construction contracting proceeds according to laws enacted by Congress and regulations drafted by the government agencies involved with procuring services and supplies. These laws and regulations are published and revised periodically. A government construction contractor must be familiar with the myriad government regulations that form the framework of construction contract administration.

Federal Acquisition Regulation

Perhaps the most important regulation is the Federal Acquisition Regulation, often referred to as the "FAR", which governs the procurement process. This regulation replaces the former Defense Acquisition Regulation (DAR), which in turn replaced the Armed Services Procurement Regulation (ASPR) and the civilian agencies' Federal Procurement Regulation (FPR). The principal parts of the FAR are listed in Figure 2.1.

Although it is impossible to be familiar with every section of the FAR, contractors and their attorneys often become experts in particular sections where problems most commonly arise. It is not sufficient, however, to research a regulatory issue by *only* looking at the FAR. Although the FAR is the controlling regulation, it is supplemented by a number of department and agency regulations which, while they cannot contradict the FAR, add to its requirements in areas where the FAR is open to interpretation. The agencies listed in Figure 2.2 have established such supplemental regulations.

Supplemental Regulations
The supplemental regulations use the same organization and numbering system as the FAR. Therefore, a contractor with a question of interpretation about a particular FAR section who needs to review the appropriate agency regulations need only search for the same numbered section and subsection in the supplemental regulations. If the agency regulation does not contain a corresponding section to the FAR, then the FAR section is the only applicable regulation. In the case of a Department of Defense contract, there are times when two or

Contents of the Federal Acquisition Regulation

Part 1 Federal Acquisition Regulation System
Part 2 Definitions of Words and Terms
Part 3 Improper Business Practices and Personal Conflicts of Interest
Part 4 Administrative Matters
Part 5 Publicizing Contract Actions
Part 6 Competition Requirements
Part 7 Acquisition Planning
Part 8 Required Sources of Supplies and Services
Part 9 Contractor Qualifications
Part 10 Specifications Standards and other Purchase Descriptions
Part 11 Acquisition and Distribution of Commercial Products
Part 12 Contract Delivery or Performance
Part 13 Small Purchase and Other Simplified Purchase Procedures
Part 14 Sealed Bidding
Part 15 Contracting by Negotiation
Part 16 Types of Contracts
Part 17 Special Contracting Methods
Part 18 [Reserved]
Part 19 Small Business and Small Disadvantaged Business Concerns
Part 20 Labor Surplus Area Concerns
Part 21 [Reserved]
Part 22 Application of Labor Laws to Government Acquisitions
Part 23 Environment, Conservation, and Occupational Safety
Part 24 Protection of Privacy and Freedom of Information
Part 25 Foreign Acquisition
Part 26 [Reserved]
Part 27 Patents, Data, and Copyrights
Part 28 Bonds and Insurance
Part 29 Taxes
Part 30 Cost Accounting Standards
Part 31 Contract Cost Principles and Procedures
Part 32 Contract Financing
Part 33 Protests, Disputes, and Appeals
Part 34 Major System Acquisition
Part 35 Research and Development Contracting
Part 36 Construction and Architect-Engineer Contracts
Part 37 Service Contracting
Part 38 Federal Supply Schedule Contracting
Part 39 Management, Acquisition, and Use of Information Resources
Part 40 [Reserved]
Part 41 [Reserved]
Part 42 Contract Administration
Part 43 Contract Modifications
Part 44 Subcontracting Policies and Procedures
Part 45 Government Property
Part 46 Quality Assurance
Part 47 Transportation
Part 48 Value Engineering
Part 49 Termination of Contracts
Part 50 Extraordinary Contractual Actions
Part 51 Use of Government Sources by Contractors
Part 52 Solicitation Provisions and Contract Clauses
Part 53 Forms

Figure 2.1

three supplemental regulations will apply. For example, if a contract is with the Corps of Engineers, three regulations are applicable (in descending order):

- Department of Defense FAR Supplement Regulation
- Service Regulation (Air Force, Army, Navy)
- Engineer FARS Regulation

However, if a contract is with the Coast Guard, only the Department of Transportation Acquisition Regulation is applicable. A number of agencies have regulations for construction contracting. A contractor must be aware that these regulations exist and that they may have an impact on contract interpretation and performance.

Competition in Contracting Act (CICA)

The Competition in Contracting Act (CICA) of 1984 [41 U.S.C. 253] revised the FAR to encourage competition for the award of all types of government contracts. The intent of the CICA is to increase the number of bids or proposals competing for government contracts by publicizing contracting opportunities. The goal is to increase government savings through lower, more competitive pricing. The CICA requires that for all contracts expected to exceed $25,000, the contracting agency must publish the proposed contracts in the *Commerce Business Daily*.

Agencies with Supplemental Regulations

Agency	Supplement
Defense Department (DOD)	DOD FAR Supplement
Air Force	Air Force Federal Acquisition Regulation Supplement
Army	Army Federal Acquisition Regulation Supplement
Corps of Engineers	Engineer FARS (EFARS)
Navy	Navy Acquisition Regulation Supplement
Defense Logistics Agency	Defense Logistics Acquisition Regulation Supplement
General Services Administration (GSA)	General Services Administration Acquisition Regulation
Department of Energy (DOE)	DOE Acquisition Regulation
Department of Transportation (DOT)	DOT Acquisition Regulation
National Aeronautics and Space Administration (NASA)	NASA FAR Supplements
Veterans Administration (VA)	VA Acquisition Regulation (VAARS)

Figure 2.2

Currently, the notices must be published at least 15 days before the issuance of a solicitation for bids. The elements of CICA are embodied in Part 6 of the FAR and apply to all solicitations for bids issued after April 1, 1985. The policy of the Act is stated below.

> Contracting officers shall provide for full and open competition through the use of the competitive procedure or combination of competitive procedures contained in this subpart that is best suited to the circumstances of the contract action. [FAR 6.101]

The requirements of the two most commonly used competitive acquisition methods, *sealed bidding* and *competitive proposals*, are outlined in the CICA (see Chapter 1, "Bidding Government Construction Projects"). Federal agencies are required to allow at least 30 days response time between issuing the solicitation and receiving bids (sealed bidding) or proposals (competitive proposals). [FAR 5.203]

Full and Open Competition

The CICA requires the government to obtain full and open competition, with only a few exceptions. The agencies are not permitted to use sole-source procurements unless the written authorization of the agency head is obtained *and* specific statutory or regulatory authority exists for sole-source or limited competition. Every deviation from the requirement for full and open competition must be documented in writing and authorized by the appropriate government official. As a result, agencies rarely seek to limit competition.

The CICA requires each agency to establish a *competition advocate* within its organization to review and challenge any procurement activity that limits competition. At the Congressional level, a Senate subcommittee was established to oversee implementation of the Act and to encourage competition for government contracts.

Amendment to Protest Procedures

The CICA also amended the protest procedures that are contained in Part 33 of the FAR. Specifically, the CICA established that a protest filed with the General Accounting Office (GAO) before contract award will cause the award to be suspended until the GAO rules on the protest. It also established a deadline of 90 business days by which time the GAO must issue a ruling — or 45 calendar days if this option is requested by either party (see Chapter 1, "Bidding Government Construction Projects").

Prompt Payment Act

One of the most significant acts passed by Congress in the past decade affecting government contracting is the Prompt Payment Act of 1982. [31 U.S.C. §3901-3906] Under the Act, the government must make contract payments within 15 days after the required payment date. The required payment date is 30 days after the government receives a proper invoice. If the government fails to make the payment in the required time, it must pay the contractor an interest penalty. If the government fails to pay the interest, then the contractor may submit a claim for the interest under the Contract Disputes Act, which is discussed later in this chapter. [41 U.S.C. §601 et seq.]

Construction Contract Progress Payments

The Prompt Payment Act was implemented by the government through the Office of Management and Budget (OMB). [Circular A-125] Initially, the OMB interpreted the Act as not applying to construction contract progress payments. However, two recent decisions of the Armed Services Board of Contract Appeals (ASBCA) have held that the Prompt Payment Act does apply to progress payments. The OMB circular has been revised accordingly to be used as a guide to government agencies with construction contracts. [See *Zinger Construction Co., Inc.*, ASBCA 31858 and *Batteast Construction Co., Inc.*, ASBCA 34420]. The government now has a financial incentive to make timely progress payments to construction contractors.

Submission of Proper Invoice

A construction contractor must submit a "proper invoice" in order to invoke the Prompt Payment Act. OMB Circular A-125 defines a proper invoice as "a bill or written request for payment . . . for property or services rendered." The invoice must include the information listed in Figure 2.3.

Upon submission of a proper invoice, the government must process the payment within 45 days of receipt (30 days plus the 15-day grace period), or pay interest. The interest is based on a rate set semiannually by the Secretary of the Treasury. If the government owes interest on a late payment, that interest accrues until the payment is made. Interest penalties unpaid for any 30-day period are added to the principal; then interest accrues on both the previous unpaid payment and the unpaid interest.

Information Required for a Proper Invoice

- Name of business
- Date of invoice
- Contract number
- Description, price, and quantity of property and/or services actually rendered
- Any payment or shipping terms
- Any documentation required by the specific contract that must accompany an invoice (e.g., labor reports, updated CPM, cash-loaded CPM)
- Name, title, phone number, and complete mailing address (if practicable) of responsible official to whom payment is to be sent

Figure 2.3

Proposed Amendments

Many federal agencies have used loopholes in the Prompt Payment Act in order to avoid making timely payments or having interest assessed. To eliminate some of these loopholes, the Senate has proposed a bill amending the Act.

Date of Invoice and Penalties

The proposed amendments to the Act define *receipt of invoice* as the later of either the date on which the invoice was sent to the first government office designated to receive it, or five days after final performance of the services rendered. The Senate bill reduces the grace period from 15 days after the required payment date to seven days, until October 1, 1989, when the grace period is eliminated entirely. The bill also provides for automatic penalties and double interest penalties. The latter would apply if the government failed to make the required interest payment within ten days after making a contract payment.

Payments to Subcontractors

The most controversial provision of the Senate bill is the section requiring a prime contractor to pay a subcontractor within seven days of the date on which the prime contractor was paid by the government. A prime contractor who fails to meet this requirement must pay interest to the subcontractor. If this bill is passed and signed into law, it will correct some of the abuses by federal agencies of the Prompt Payment Act. It will also aid the contracting industry by promoting better financial management, and will affect the manner in which prime contractors deal with their subcontractors.

Davis-Bacon Act

Congress passed the Davis-Bacon Act in 1931 [40 U.S.C. 276(a)] in order to establish minimum wages for various job classifications on all federal construction projects in excess of two thousand dollars. The statute requires that every laborer and mechanic on the site will be paid not less than the "prevailing wages" determined by the Secretary of Labor. The prevailing wages are based on Department of Labor surveys in specified locations for the various trades. These wages are included in the solicitation for bids and apply throughout the life of the contract. Contractors must pay these wages as a minimum. Presently, there are bills in Congress seeking to have the two thousand dollar threshold raised to one hundred thousand or one million dollars in an effort to reduce government costs and paperwork.

Both the Department of Labor and the federal agency may conduct audits and interviews to determine if the proper wages are being paid. In the event a discrepancy or underpayment is found, the contractor will be requested to make restitution and to furnish evidence that such restitution has been made. A contractor who fails to comply with these labor standards runs the risk of having monies withheld and possibly having the company and its officers debarred, i.e., suspended for a period of up to three years from receiving another government contract.

Miller Act

In an effort to protect all persons furnishing labor and materials on federal contracts, Congress enacted the Miller Act. [40 U.S.C. §270a-e] On any contract exceeding $25,000, the prime contractor must furnish the government with a performance bond and a payment bond. The performance bond must be for the full amount of the contract, and the payment bond must be 50 percent of the contract amount if the contract is less than one million dollars, 40 percent for contracts from one to five million dollars, and a flat 2.5 million dollars for all contracts over five million dollars.

The performance and payment bonds, obtained from a surety or sureties acceptable to the government, are furnished by the contractor prior to the *Notice to Proceed* (with the contract work). The sole purpose of the performance bond is to protect the government by insuring completion of the project.

Subcontractors and Laborers

According to the Miller Act, every person who has furnished labor or material and who has not been paid in full by the end of a 90-day period following completion of the last work or material delivery, can sue on the payment bond. A *first-tier subcontractor* is fully protected by the payment bond as long as the suit is filed within *one year* of the date after the last work was performed or material was furnished.

To be protected by the Miller Act and paid under the terms of the payment bond, a laborer or supplier who has a direct contractual relationship with a first-tier subcontractor must provide the prime contractor with written notice within 90 days of the date the last work was performed or material furnished. The laborer or supplier in this situation must also file suit within the one-year requirement described above. When furnishing written notice to the prime contractor, it is advisable to send a copy to the contractor's bonding company.

Mechanic's Liens

One of the effects of the Miller Act is to remove the common-law remedy of filing a mechanic's lien. A mechanic's lien is a legal means of securing payment for work performed or materials furnished. A lien attaches land, buildings, and improvements, any of which may be sold to satisfy the lien. These liens are unacceptable on federal projects because the government cannot have its property sold to pay debts owed to contractors. Contractors must instead rely on the remedies provided by the Miller Act. It is imperative that subcontractors on a federal construction project be aware of the rights and duties of all parties under the Miller Act in order to be protected if payment is not received.

Freedom of Information Act

The Acts which we have presented thus far in this chapter concern competition, wages, and prompt payment. The Freedom of Information Act [(FOIA) (5 U.S.C. 552)] has a different purpose. (For information on use of the FOIA in government contracting, see Chapter 10). Under the Freedom of Information Act, persons may request copies of records maintained by a federal agency. Agencies must release these records to the requester upon payment of copy and search fees, unless an applicable exemption permits denial of the request. The statutory exemptions to the Freedom of Information Act are listed in Figure 2.4. The most commonly invoked exemptions are *privileged or confidential information* and *inter- and intra-agency correspondence*. A construction contractor can utilize the FOIA to obtain agency records on a variety of items that may support a claim. FOIA records can also provide a defense to actions by the agency, or provide insight into contract interpretation or administration.

Requirements

A request made under the FOIA should reference the Act and should indicate that reasonable fees for document review and copying will be paid. Some federal agencies may require the payment to be made in advance of receipt of the documents. If a large number of documents are sought, it is advisable to request permission to review the documents in order to select those that will need to be copied. Most agencies cooperate with such requests and will make the requested documents available at a mutually convenient time. It is also important to request a list of any documents withheld by the agency in order to determine whether a basis exists for an appeal.

Buy American Act

The Buy American Act [41 U.S.C. 10] and the attendant Executive Order 10582 (December 17, 1954) as amended, essentially require that only domestic construction materials be used in government construction projects — unless this use is inconsistent with the public interest or the cost is unreasonable.

Statutory Exemptions to the Freedom of Information Act

- National defense or foreign policy matters classified as such by executive order.
- Matters relating solely to the internal personnel rules or practices of an agency.
- Statutory exemptions.
- Trade secrets and commercial or financial information that is obtained from a person and is privileged or confidential.
- Interagency or intra-agency memorandums or letters.
- Personnel, medical, or similar files which would clearly be an unwarranted invasion of privacy.
- Law enforcement investigative records.
- Reports regarding operation of financial institutions.
- Geological and geophysical information, including maps for wells.

Figure 2.4

Only unmanufactured articles, materials, and supplies that have been mined or produced in the United States and only articles, materials, and supplies that have been manufactured in the United States substantially from articles, materials, or supplies mined, produced, or manufactured in the United States shall be acquired for public use. (Part 25.2 of the Federal Acquisition Regulation also applies to contracts for the construction, alteration, or repair of any public building or public work in the United States.)

Domestic Construction Material

The definition of a *domestic construction material* is (1) an unmanufactured construction material mined or produced in the United States or (2) a construction material manufactured in the United States if the cost of its components mined, produced, or manufactured in the United States exceeds 50 percent of the cost of all of its components. To determine whether a particular construction material complies with the Buy American Act, it must be known whether or not the material is *manufactured* in the United States. Use of a material that is not manufactured in the United States is a violation of the Act, unless some other exception applies. A material is considered manufactured in the United States if 50 percent of the cost of its components are mined, produced, or manufactured in the United States.

Exceptions

The Buy American Act requires the use of only domestic construction materials for government construction projects in the United States, except under one of the following conditions:

- The cost would be unreasonable (as determined in accordance with FAR 25.203).
- The federal agency involved determined that use of a particular domestic construction material would be impracticable.
- One or more agencies have determined that the construction material is not available, i.e., mined, produced, or manufactured in the United States in sufficient and reasonably available commercial quantities of a satisfactory quality. [FAR 25.202]

Violations and Waivers

An intentional violation of the Buy American Act may result in the debarment of a contractor for a period of up to three years. It is possible, however, to obtain a waiver of the Buy American Act upon application to the head of the agency involved. If possible, applications for a waiver should be made prior to bidding.

Equal Access to Justice Act

The Equal Access to Justice Act [5 U.S.C. §504] was enacted by Congress to enable small businesses to receive compensation for attorneys' fees and expenses incurred in connection with contract claims and appeals. There are various criteria and limitations regarding the application of the Act for the recovery of fees. A few of the provisions for a construction contractor to be aware of are discussed briefly below.

- The Act applies to individuals with a net worth of not more than two million dollars, or unincorporated businesses, partnerships, or corporations with a net worth of not more than seven million dollars and 500 employees.
- An application for recovery of fees may be made only if the applicant was the prevailing party and it is found that the government's position was not substantially justified.
- Recovery is limited to reasonable, allocable fees and expenses. Recovery of attorneys' fees is limited to $75 per hour, regardless of the actual legal fees incurred.
- Contractors who appear *pro se* (i.e., represent themselves) cannot recover legal fees under the Act.
- Application must be made within 30 days of the decision on the claim.

There are many other requirements and issues connected with The Equal Access to Justice Act. A contractor who meets the size standards noted above and wants to file an application should review the Act with counsel. Recovery under the Act has been limited, but contractors should be aware of its provisions and applicability.

Contract Disputes Act of 1978

The Contract Disputes Act of 1978 [41 U.S.C. 601 et seq.] revised the disputes procedure and established a number of requirements for government contract claims. The Act permits the contractor to recover interest on claims and establishes durations for government processing of claims and for filing appeals from contracting officer decisions. The essence of the Disputes Act is set forth in Part 33 of the Federal Acquisition Regulation.

Chapter Three
The Contract Package and Significant Clauses

Chapter Three
The Contract Package and Significant Clauses

The solicitation and award of a federal government construction contract is controlled by a variety of laws and regulations. The purpose of these laws is to regulate the way in which federal agencies spend the taxpayers' money. These rules determine procurement practices, and also carry out a number of social policies involving minority and disadvantaged businesses, small business concerns, and protection of American industry. Together, these requirements make up an extremely fair and equitable system for acquiring contractor services.

Almost all federal construction contracts are awarded on a firm fixed-price basis using the sealed bid acquisition method. This method presumes that all bidders have a common understanding of the requirements of the plans and specifications, and that the lowest bidder will be awarded the contract. Unfortunately, the complicated nature of many construction projects makes it difficult for project designers to anticipate all potential construction problems, and procuring agencies are often forced to decide which contract interpretation is the most reasonable. The growing extent to which post-award interpretations and construction problems affect contract price or result in disputes makes it imperative that all parties have a common understanding of the project requirements prior to bidding, and certainly before award of the contract. It is extremely important, therefore, that bidders understand the organization and content of federal construction contracts. Figure 3.1 shows the general organization of a contract package. The following pages contain discussions of the forms and clauses that make up a typical government contract.

Organization of the Contract

Solicitation, Offer, Award
Federal agencies subject to the Federal Acquisition Regulation use a set of standardized forms for organizing and issuing construction contracts. (The Post Office, Federal Pension Benefit Guaranty Corporation, and some other agencies are not governed by the FAR.) This contract package includes Standard Form 1442, *Solicitation, Offer, Award*, shown in Figure 3.2 at the end of this chapter. The following information is recorded on this

form: the project title, contract number, appropriation data, time for receipt of bids, performance period, acknowledgment of amendments, contract price, and, most importantly, the signatures of the contractor and the contracting officer. This

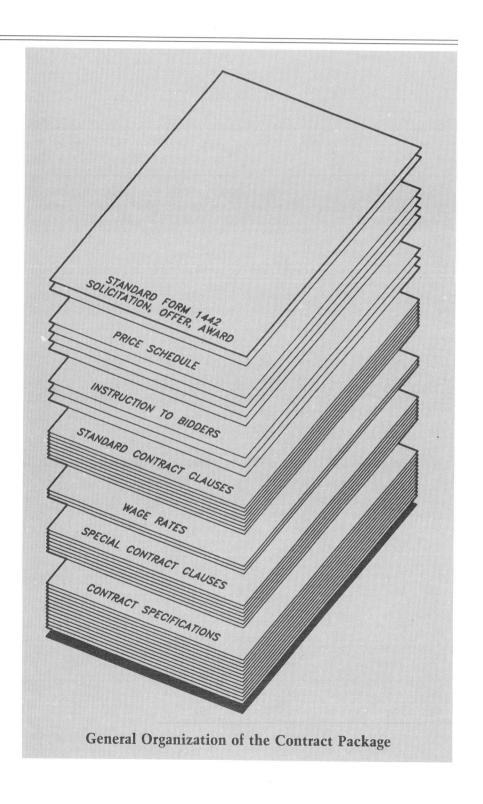

General Organization of the Contract Package

Figure 3.1

document is included in the bid solicitation and ultimately becomes the first page of the contract.

Instructions
The contract package also contains instructions on how contractors are to prepare the bid. These instructions are in a series of "Representations and Certifications" covering items such as business organization, small business status, affirmative action, and environmental matters.

Standard Clauses
Usually, the next portion of the contract package is the standard or general contract clauses from the Federal Acquisition Regulations (described later in this chapter). There may be from 25 to 70 of these clauses, depending upon the agency, the contract, and the implementing regulations.

Wage Rates
The contract package for every construction contract over $2,000 must include published wage decisions as specified by the Davis-Bacon Act. These wage rates represent the minimum which the contractor must pay for various job classifications. Wage rates are sometimes added to the solicitation in the form of an amendment before bidding begins. In this way, the most up-to-date rates can be assured. Regardless of whether the wage rate information is included in the contract package, or as an amendment to the solicitation, the contractor is obligated to pay these specified wages as a minimum for the trades listed.

Special Clauses
Agencies usually include a set of special contract clauses. These may vary from agency to agency, but generally include clauses regarding performance time, liquidated damages, scheduling (CPM, bar chart, NAS), warranty of construction, and insurance required for the contract. This section also contains clauses specific to the project, such as the designated work hours at the site, security and disposal requirements, location of office and storage trailers, and safety procedures.

Specifications
The last major section of the contract package contains the technical provisions or specifications. The specifications are divided into sections or divisions, such as earthwork, concrete, structural steel, miscellaneous steel, painting, mechanical, exterior electrical, and interior electrical. These divisions are further broken down into subdivisions. When all of these items are bound together, contractors are presented with a contract package containing all of the provisions necessary to understand and perform the job. The contractor should fully understand the contract terms and conditions before submitting the bid.

Standard Forms

Many agencies use a standard contract clause package, included as part of the contract. For example, the Corps of Engineers publishes and distributes nationwide standard contract packages for construction, supply, and service contracts. The following paragraphs describe the forms that are typically included in the contract package.

- Standard Form 1442 (SF 1442), *Solicitation, Offer, Award*. This form lists pertinent contract data and is executed by both parties as the first page of the contract. This form is shown in Figure 3.2 at the end of this chapter.
- Standard Form 30, *Amendment of Solicitation/Modification of Contract*. This form is used for the procurement of small purchases and/or modifications to a contract that is awarded by the sealed bidding method. It provides spaces for both the contractor and the government Contracting Officer to sign, signifying agreement to the terms on the face of the form and the attached or incorporated documents. This form is shown in Figure 3.3 at the end of this chapter.
- SF 24, *Bid Bond*. The bond forms describe the bonding requirements for a project. Each bid over $25,000 must be accompanied by a bid bond or other acceptable guarantee. If a corporate surety is used, the contractor and its surety should complete SF 24, *Bid Bond*. While a contractor is not required to use this form for corporate sureties, it is recommended. If SF 24 is not used, the government may question the substituted forms, which could lead to disqualification of the contractor. This form is shown in Figure 3.4 at the end of this chapter.

The proper execution of bid bonds is critical since the bidder may be disqualified if the bid bond does not comply with the requirements of the solicitation. Bidders should verify that bid bonds are properly signed and dated, are in the proper amount, and identify the proper solicitation and agency.

- SF 25, *Performance Bond* and SF 25-A, *Payment Bond*. After the contract is awarded, the contractor must submit performance and payment bonds for all construction contracts over $25,000. Federal agencies use SF 25, *Performance Bond* and SF 25-A, *Payment Bond* to meet these requirements. It is to the contractor's advantage to use these forms as most corporate sureties are familiar with the forms and with the rights and obligations printed on them. These forms are shown in Figures 3.5 and 3.6 at the end of this chapter.
- SF 1411, *Contract Pricing Proposal Cover Sheet*. Contractors may also be required to complete and execute SF 1411, *Contract Pricing Proposal Cover Sheet*. The Federal Acquisition Regulations require cost or pricing data on price proposals for modifications in excess of $100,000, including credits. This pricing data should include all financial information available at the time of the price agreement that may significantly affect or influence price negotiations. Cost or pricing information must be in the form of verifiable, factual data. The government agencies review this form and may utilize it when auditing the contractor's price proposal. Furthermore, the contractor's certification of current cost or prices must be accurate, as defective data could be used against the contractor. This form is shown in Figure 3.7 at the end of this chapter.

Significant Clauses

There are many clauses in government contracts, and contractors should be aware of each of them. There are, however, ten clauses that stand out, since they cover ninety percent of the problem areas encountered in construction contracts. Each of these clauses is included in every federal construction contract. They are described individually in the following sections.

Changes

According to the FAR, the changes clause permits the government to make "changes in the general scope of the contract." This clause also requires that the government make an equitable adjustment in the contract price for modifications to the drawings, specifications, materials, or method of performance.

The Changes Clause also permits the contractor to assert that a change has occurred if the government gives any written or oral order (such as an instruction, interpretation, or direction) that causes a change to the contract. This concept is known as a *constructive change*. Contractors should be aware of the occurrence of constructive changes. (See Chapter 5 for detailed coverage of constructive changes.) If a contractor believes that an oral or written statement by government representatives has caused a change in the work, it should notify the government *in writing* of the change. The contractor should then keep track of the costs incurred as a result of this change and request an equitable adjustment in the contract price. Under the language of the clause, these changes are treated as if the government ordered the change, entitling the contractor to an equitable adjustment.

Differing Site Conditions

This clause places the risk of unforeseen site conditions on the government. With this clause included in the contract, contractors do not have to place contingencies in their bids for unknown subsurface or other physical site conditions. There are two types of differing site conditions, sometimes referred to as *Type I* and *Type II*.

Type I

Type I are physical conditions which differ materially from those indicated in the contract. For a contractor to receive compensation for a differing site condition, the condition must differ materially from what was described in the contract in the form of specification language, boring logs, drawings, or a description of soils. An example of a *Type I* condition is boring logs that do not indicate rock later encountered by the contractor. The rock that is encountered may require more extensive excavation efforts than those specified in the contract.

Type II

According to the FAR, a Type II differing site condition is defined as "unknown physical conditions of an unusual nature which differ materially from those ordinarily encountered and generally recognized as inhering in work of the character provided for in the contract." An example of a Type II condition is encountering a subsurface structure in an area which appeared to contain soil only.

The Differing Site Conditions Clause requires that the contractor promptly notify the government (preferably in writing) of the condition and that the affected area not be disturbed before the government representatives have investigated it. The government must investigate the condition and direct the contractor as to what to do about the condition. This clause, with respect to changes to the contract, is further discussed in Chapter 5.

Disputes Clause

The Disputes Clause states that the contractor must proceed with the contract even if there is a dispute for which the contractor has made a claim. If the contractor disagrees with the government's interpretation of what the contract requires, that interpretation must still be followed until the claim is addressed. The job should never be abandoned or work halted while waiting for the claim to be addressed. Stopping work puts the contractor at risk for termination based on default. (This clause is discussed in more detail in Chapter 10.)

Termination for Convenience

The Termination for Convenience Clause allows the government to terminate the contract in writing when it is in the best interest of the government to do so. The government may terminate part or all of the contract, and may do so at any stage of the project. For example, this clause may be exercised if a contractor performing rehabilitation of government housing discovers that the buildings are termite-infested. The government may determine that repairs would exceed cost limits and may, therefore, choose to terminate the contract for its convenience. The contractor can recover costs expended and a profit up to the date of termination. However, the loss of future profits cannot be recovered. This kind of termination is not considered a "black mark" on the contractor's record and does not affect his performance evaluation. Contractors should be careful not to agree to "no cost" terminations for convenience, however, and should insist on receiving an equitable adjustment according to the terms of the termination clause.

Default

This clause permits the government to terminate the contract if the contractor fails to perform *on time, with the diligence to insure timely completion,* or *in accordance with the requirements of the contract.* The government has the right to complete the work and charge the contractor for any excess costs incurred following a termination for default. Both the contractor and its surety would be liable for these costs.

The Default Clause also provides for time extensions to the contract if the contractor is delayed by "unforeseeable causes beyond its control and without any negligence or fault by the contractor." [FAR] Some examples of excusable delays are strikes, unusually severe weather, floods, fires, and acts of the government (war, embargo, etc.). A time extension for these delays is granted to the contractor, but not compensation for the delays. This issue is discussed in more detail in Chapter 6.

Suspension of Work

This clause allows the government to order the contractor to stop or suspend work for a "reasonable" period of time without cost to the government. If a stop work order is in effect for an unreasonable period of time, then an adjustment is made in the contract price. For this reason, it is important for the contractor to keep track of costs incurred during the suspension period. The clause, however, prohibits the contractor from adding a profit percentage to the compensation costs. Notice must be provided *within 20 days* if a compensation claim is to be filed under this clause.

Inspection of Construction

This clause obligates the contractor to an inspection of the work to ensure that the structure conforms to the contract requirements. This arrangement is known as the *quality control system*. The government may inspect the site at any reasonable time before acceptance in order to ensure compliance with the contract. However, the presence of a government representative does not relieve the contractor of the responsibility to comply with the inspection requirements of the contract.

The inspection clause also obligates the contractor to replace or correct nonconforming work at its own expense. If the contractor fails to do so, the government may take corrective action and either charge the contractor for the costs or terminate the contract for default.

The other important feature of this clause concerns *acceptance*. The government should accept the work as promptly as possible. That acceptance is considered final and conclusive unless the government proves that the work contains latent defects, was fraudulently performed, or contains gross mistakes which amount to fraud. Under those circumstances, the acceptance is defunct, and the contractor must correct or replace the items.

Materials and Workmanship

This clause requires that all materials be new and that all work be performed in a professional manner. It also allows the contractor to substitute an "equal" item for any item specified by brand name, model number, or catalog description in the contract, unless it is specifically indicated that only the specified item will be accepted.

Permits and Responsibilities

This provision states that the contractor is obligated to obtain all necessary permits and licenses for the project, and to comply with any applicable federal, state, or local law, code, or regulation. This broadly-worded provision also obligates the contractor to pay for damages due to negligence and any damages to the work itself prior to acceptance by the government. The government often cites this clause in denying contractor claims pertaining to sales taxes, sediment control, burning permits, and/or utility inspections.

Progress Payments

The government, under direction of this clause, makes monthly progress payments based on the estimated completion of the work. This clause also permits the government to make payments for materials delivered, but not yet incorporated into the work. Upon completion and acceptance of all the work, the government must pay the remaining amount due. Usually, the final payment is accompanied by a release of all claims against the government which the contractor must sign. This release should not be signed if the contractor has outstanding claims, as a signed release may deny the contractor the right to file any further claims for additional time or money.

The clauses that we have described in this last section are the most significant in government construction contracts, as they cover most of the areas in which problems tend to arise. There are, however, many other clauses relating to such matters as labor, safety, affirmative action, warranties, scheduling and subcontractors. The contractor should be familiar with these other clauses as well before submitting a bid, since they may impact the cost or manner of performing the work.

SOLICITATION, OFFER, AND AWARD *(Construction, Alteration, or Repair)*	1. SOLICITATION NO.	2. TYPE OF SOLICITATION ☐ SEALED BID *(IFB)* ☐ NEGOTIATED *(RFP)*	3. DATE ISSUED	PAGE OF PAGES

IMPORTANT — The "offer" section on the reverse must be fully completed by offeror.

4. CONTRACT NO.	5. REQUISITION/PURCHASE REQUEST NO.	6. PROJECT NO.

7. ISSUED BY	CODE	8. ADDRESS OFFER TO

9. FOR INFORMATION CALL: ▶	A. NAME	B. TELEPHONE NO. *(Include area code)* *(NO COLLECT CALLS)*

SOLICITATION

NOTE: In sealed bid solicitations "offer" and "offeror" mean "bid" and "bidder".

10. THE GOVERNMENT REQUIRES PERFORMANCE OF THE WORK DESCRIBED IN THESE DOCUMENTS *(Title, identifying no., date)*:

11. The Contractor shall begin performance within _____ calendar days and complete it within _____ calendar days after receiving ☐ award, ☐ notice to proceed This performance period is ☐ mandatory, ☐ negotiable *(See _____ .)*

12A. THE CONTRACTOR MUST FURNISH ANY REQUIRED PERFORMANCE AND PAYMENT BONDS? *(If "YES," indicate within how many calendar days after award in Item 12B.)* ☐ YES ☐ NO	12B. CALENDAR DAYS

13. ADDITIONAL SOLICITATION REQUIREMENTS:

A. Sealed offers in original and _____ copies to perform the work required are due at the place specified in Item 8 by _____ *(hour)* local time _____ *(date)*. If this is a sealed bid solicitation, offers will be publicly opened at that time. Sealed envelopes containing offers shall be marked to show the offeror's name and address, the solicitation number, and the date and time offers are due.

B. An offer guarantee ☐ is, ☐ is not required.

C. All offers are subject to the (1) work requirements, and (2) other provisions and clauses incorporated in the solicitation in full text or by reference.

D. Offers providing less than _____ calendar days for Government acceptance after the date offers are due will not be considered and will be rejected

NSN 7540-01-155-3212   THIS PUBLICATION IS A COURTESY QUICK COPY FROM THE BALTIMORE ARMY PUBLICATIONS CENTER TO MEET YOUR NEEDS WHILE WE ARE REPLENISHING OUR REGULAR STOCK.   1442-102   STANDARD FORM 1442 (REV. 4-85)
Prescribed by GSA
FAR (48 CFR) 53.236-1(d)

Figure 3.2

OFFER (Must be fully completed by offeror)

14. NAME AND ADDRESS OF OFFEROR (Include ZIP Code)	15. TELEPHONE NO. (Include area code)
	16. REMITTANCE ADDRESS (Include only if different than Item 14)
CODE FACILITY CODE	

17 The offeror agrees to perform the work required at the prices specified below in strict accordance with the terms of this solicitation, if this offer is accepted by the Government in writing within _____ calendar days after the date offers are due. (Insert any number equal to or greater than the minimum requirement stated in Item 13D. Failure to insert any number means the offeror accepts the minimum in Item 13D.

AMOUNTS ▶

18. The offeror agrees to furnish any required performance and payment bonds.

19. ACKNOWLEDGMENT OF AMENDMENTS
(The offeror acknowledges receipt of amendments to the solicitation — give number and date of each)

AMENDMENT NO.								
DATE								

20A. NAME AND TITLE OF PERSON AUTHORIZED TO SIGN OFFER (Type or print)	20B. SIGNATURE	20C. OFFER DATE

AWARD (To be completed by Government)

21. ITEMS ACCEPTED:

22. AMOUNT	23. ACCOUNTING AND APPROPRIATION DATA

24 SUBMIT INVOICES TO ADDRESS SHOWN IN (4 copies unless otherwise specified) ▶ ITEM	25. OTHER THAN FULL AND OPEN COMPETITION PURSUANT TO ☐ 10 U.S.C. 2304(c) ( ) ☐ 41 U.S.C. 253(c) ( )
26. ADMINISTERED BY CODE	27. PAYMENT WILL BE MADE BY

CONTRACTING OFFICER WILL COMPLETE ITEM 28 OR 29 AS APPLICABLE

☐ 28 NEGOTIATED AGREEMENT Contractor is required to sign this document and return _____ copies to issuing office.) Contractor agrees to furnish and deliver all items or perform all work requirements identified on this form and any continuation sheets for the consideration stated in this contract. The rights and obligations of the parties to this contract shall be governed by (a) this contract award, (b) the solicitation, and (c) the clauses, representations, certifications, and specifications incorporated by reference in or attached to this contract	☐ 29. AWARD (Contractor is not required to sign this document.) Your offer on this solicitation is hereby accepted as to the items listed. This award consummates the contract, which consists of (a) the Government solicitation and your offer, and (b) this contract award. No further contractual document is necessary.
30A. NAME AND TITLE OF CONTRACTOR OR PERSON AUTHORIZED TO SIGN (Type or print)	31A. NAME OF CONTRACTING OFFICER (Type or print)
30B. SIGNATURE 30C. DATE	31B. UNITED STATES OF AMERICA 31C. AWARD DATE BY

☆ U.S. Government Printing Office: 1985—477-664/30131

STANDARD FORM 1442 BACK (REV. 4-85

US ARMY   PUBLICATIONS CENTER
BALTIMORE – 1985

Figure 3.2 (cont.)

AMENDMENT OF SOLICITATION/MODIFICATION OF CONTRACT

1. CONTRACT ID CODE	PAGE OF PAGES

2. AMENDMENT/MODIFICATION NO.	3. EFFECTIVE DATE	4. REQUISITION/PURCHASE REQ. NO.	5. PROJECT NO. (If applicable)

6. ISSUED BY CODE	7. ADMINISTERED BY (If other than Item 6) CODE

8. NAME AND ADDRESS OF CONTRACTOR (No., street, county, State and ZIP Code)	(√)	9A. AMENDMENT OF SOLICITATION NO.
		9B. DATED (SEE ITEM 11)
		10A. MODIFICATION OF CONTRACT/ORDER NO.
		10B. DATED (SEE ITEM 13)

CODE	FACILITY CODE

11. THIS ITEM ONLY APPLIES TO AMENDMENTS OF SOLICITATIONS

☐ The above numbered solicitation is amended as set forth in Item 14. The hour and date specified for receipt of Offers ☐ is extended, ☐ is not extended.

Offers must acknowledge receipt of this amendment prior to the hour and date specified in the solicitation or as amended, by one of the following methods:

(a) By completing Items 8 and 15, and returning _____ copies of the amendment; (b) By acknowledging receipt of this amendment on each copy of the offer submitted; or (c) By separate letter or telegram which includes a reference to the solicitation and amendment numbers. FAILURE OF YOUR ACKNOWLEDGMENT TO BE RECEIVED AT THE PLACE DESIGNATED FOR THE RECEIPT OF OFFERS PRIOR TO THE HOUR AND DATE SPECIFIED MAY RESULT IN REJECTION OF YOUR OFFER. If by virtue of this amendment you desire to change an offer already submitted, such change may be made by telegram or letter, provided each telegram or letter makes reference to the solicitation and this amendment, and is received prior to the opening hour and date specified.

12. ACCOUNTING AND APPROPRIATION DATA (If required)

13. THIS ITEM APPLIES ONLY TO MODIFICATIONS OF CONTRACTS/ORDERS, IT MODIFIES THE CONTRACT/ORDER NO. AS DESCRIBED IN ITEM 14.

(√)

A. THIS CHANGE ORDER IS ISSUED PURSUANT TO: (Specify authority) THE CHANGES SET FORTH IN ITEM 14 ARE MADE IN THE CONTRACT ORDER NO. IN ITEM 10A.

B. THE ABOVE NUMBERED CONTRACT/ORDER IS MODIFIED TO REFLECT THE ADMINISTRATIVE CHANGES (such as changes in paying office, appropriation date, etc.) SET FORTH IN ITEM 14, PURSUANT TO THE AUTHORITY OF FAR 43.103(b).

C. THIS SUPPLEMENTAL AGREEMENT IS ENTERED INTO PURSUANT TO AUTHORITY OF:

D. OTHER (Specify type of modification and authority)

E. IMPORTANT: Contractor ☐ is not, ☐ is required to sign this document and return _____ copies to the issuing office.

14. DESCRIPTION OF AMENDMENT/MODIFICATION (Organized by UCF section headings, including solicitation/contract subject matter where feasible.)

Except as provided herein, all terms and conditions of the document referenced in Item 9A or 10A, as heretofore changed, remains unchanged and in full force and effect.

15A. NAME AND TITLE OF SIGNER (Type or print)	16A. NAME AND TITLE OF CONTRACTING OFFICER (Type or print)

15B. CONTRACTOR/OFFEROR	15C. DATE SIGNED	16B. UNITED STATES OF AMERICA	16C. DATE SIGNED
_____ (Signature of person authorized to sign)		BY _____ (Signature of Contracting Officer)	

NSN 7540-01-152-8070
PREVIOUS EDITION UNUSABLE

30–105–02

STANDARD FORM 30 (REV. 10-83)
Prescribed by GSA
FAR (48 CFR) 53.243

Figure 3.3

INSTRUCTIONS

Instructions for items other than those that are self-explanatory, are as follows:

(a) Item 1 (Contract ID Code). Insert the contract type identification code that appears in the title block of the contract being modified.

(b) Item 3 (Effective date).

(1) For a solicitation amendment, change order, or administrative change, the effective date shall be the issue date of the amendment, change order, or administrative change.

(2) For a supplemental agreement, the effective date shall be the date agreed to by the contracting parties.

(3) For a modification issued as an initial or confirming notice of termination for the convenience of the Government, the effective date and the modification number of the confirming notice shall be the same as the effective date and modification number of the initial notice.

(4) For a modification converting a termination for default to a termination for the convenience of the Government, the effective date shall be the same as the effective date of the termination for default.

(5) For a modification confirming the contracting officer's determination of the amount due in settlement of a contract termination, the effective date shall be the same as the effective date of the initial decision.

(c) Item 6 (Issued By). Insert the name and address of the issuing office. If applicable, insert the appropriate issuing office code in the code block.

(d) Item 8 (Name and Address of Contractor). For modifications to a contract or order, enter the contractor's name, address, and code as shown in the original contract or order, unless changed by this or a previous modification.

(e) Items 9, (Amendment of Solicitation No.–Dated), and 10, (Modification of Contract/Order No.–Dated). Check the appropriate box and in the corresponding blanks insert the number and date of the original solicitation, contract, or order.

(f) Item 12 (Accounting and Appropriation Data). When appropriate, indicate the impact of the modification on each affected accounting classification by inserting one of the following entries:

(1) Accounting classification ....
    Net increase $ ....

(2) Accounting classification ....
    Net decrease $ ....

NOTE: If there are changes to multiple accounting classifications that cannot be placed in block 12, insert an asterisk and the words "See continuation sheet".

(g) Item 13. Check the appropriate box to indicate the type of modification. Insert in the corresponding blank the authority under which the modification is issued. Check whether or not contractor must sign this document. (See FAR 43.103.)

(h) Item 14 (Description of Amendment/Modification).

(1) Organize amendments or modifications under the appropriate Uniform Contract Format (UCF) section headings from the applicable solicitation or contract. The UCF table of contents, however, shall not be set forth in this document.

(2) Indicate the impact of the modification on the overall total contract price by inserting one of the following entries:

(i) Total contract price increased by $ ....

(ii) Total contract price decreased by $ ....

(iii) Total contract price unchanged.

(3) State reason for modification.

(4) When removing, reinstating, or adding funds, identify the contract items and accounting classifications.

(5) When the SF 30 is used to reflect a determination by the contracting officer of the amount due in settlement of a contract terminated for the convenience of the Government, the entry in Item 14 of the modification may be limited to —

(i) A reference to the letter determination; and

(ii) A statement of the net amount determined to be due in settlement of the contract.

(6) Include subject matter or short title of solicitation/contract where feasible.

(i) Item 16B. The contracting officer's signature is not required on solicitation amendments. The contracting officer's signature is normally affixed last on supplemental agreements.

STANDARD FORM 30 BACK (REV. 10-83)

U.S. GOVERNMENT PRINTING OFFICE : 1985 O - 473-922

Figure 3.3 (cont.)

STANDARD FORM 24 JUNE 1964 EDITION GENERAL SERVICES ADMINISTRATION FED. PROC. REG. (41 CFR) 1-16.801	**BID BOND** *(See Instructions on reverse)*	24-103	DATE BOND EXECUTED *(Must not be later than bid opening date)*

PRINCIPAL *(Legal name and business address)*	TYPE OF ORGANIZATION *("X" one)*
	☐ INDIVIDUAL ☐ PARTNERSHIP ☐ JOINT VENTURE ☐ CORPORATION STATE OF INCORPORATION

SURETY(IES) *(Name and business address)*

PENAL SUM OF BOND					BID IDENTIFICATION	
PERCENT OF BID PRICE	AMOUNT NOT TO EXCEED				BID DATE	INVITATION NO.
	MILLION(S)	THOUSAND(S)	HUNDRED(S)	CENTS		
					FOR *(Construction, Supplies or Services)*	

KNOW ALL MEN BY THESE PRESENTS, That we, the Principal and Surety(ies) hereto, are firmly bound to the United States of America (hereinafter called the Government) in the above penal sum for the payment of which we bind ourselves, our heirs, executors, administrators, and successors, jointly and severally: *Provided,* That, where the Sureties are corporations acting as co-sureties, we, the Sureties, bind ourselves in such sum "jointly and severally" as well as "severally" only for the purpose of allowing a joint action or actions against any or all of us, and for all other purposes each Surety binds itself, jointly and severally with the Principal, for the payment of such sum only as is set forth opposite the name of such Surety, but if no limit of liability is indicated, the limit of liability shall be the full amount of the penal sum.

THE CONDITION OF THIS OBLIGATION IS SUCH, that whereas the Principal has submitted the bid identified above.

NOW, THEREFORE, if the Principal, upon acceptance by the Government of his bid identified above, within the period specified therein for acceptance (sixty (60) days if no period is specified), shall execute such further contractual documents, if any, and give such bond(s) as may be required by the terms of the bid as accepted within the time specified (ten (10) days if no period is specified) after receipt of the forms by him, or in the event of failure so to execute such further contractual documents and give such bonds, if the Principal shall pay the Government for any cost of procuring the work which exceeds the amount of his bid, then the above obligation shall be void and of no effect.

Each Surety executing this instrument hereby agrees that its obligation shall not be impaired by any extension(s) of the time for acceptance of the bid that the Principal may grant to the Government, notice of which extension(s) to the Surety(ies) being hereby waived; provided that such waiver of notice shall apply only with respect to extensions aggregating not more than sixty (60) calendar days in addition to the period originally allowed for acceptance of the bid.

IN WITNESS WHEREOF, the Principal and Surety(ies) have executed this bid bond and have affixed their seals on the date set forth above.

PRINCIPAL				
Signature(s)	1.		2.	
		(Seal)		*(Seal)*
Name(s) & Title(s) *(Typed)*	1.		2.	Corporate Seal

INDIVIDUAL SURETIES				
Signature(s)	1.	*(Seal)*	2.	*(Seal)*
Name(s) *(Typed)*	1.		2.	

CORPORATE SURETY(IES)				
SURETY A	Name & Address		STATE OF INC.	LIABILITY LIMIT
	Signature(s)	1.	2.	Corporate Seal
	Name(s) & Title(s) *(Typed)*	1.	2.	

Figure 3.4

				STATE OF INC.	LIABILITY LIMIT	
		CORPORATE SURETY(IES) (Continued)				
SURETY B	Name & Address			STATE OF INC.	LIABILITY LIMIT	*Corporate Seal*
	Signature(s)	1.	2.			
	Name(s) & Title(s) *(Typed)*	1.	2.			
SURETY C	Name & Address			STATE OF INC.	LIABILITY LIMIT	*Corporate Seal*
	Signature(s)	1.	2.			
	Name(s) & Title(s) *(Typed)*	1.	2.			
SURETY D	Name & Address			STATE OF INC.	LIABILITY LIMIT	*Corporate Seal*
	Signature(s)	1.	2.			
	Name(s) & Title(s) *(Typed)*	1.	2.			
SURETY E	Name & Address			STATE OF INC.	LIABILITY LIMIT	*Corporate Seal*
	Signature(s)	1.	2.			
	Name(s) & Title(s) *(Typed)*	1.	2.			
SURETY F	Name & Address			STATE OF INC.	LIABILITY LIMIT	*Corporate Seal*
	Signature(s)	1.	2.			
	Name(s) & Title(s) *(Typed)*	1.	2.			
SURETY G	Name & Address			STATE OF INC.	LIABILITY LIMIT	*Corporate Seal*
	Signature(s)	1.	2.			
	Name(s) & Title(s) *(Typed)*	1.	2.			

INSTRUCTIONS

1. This form is authorized for use whenever a bid guaranty is required in connection with construction work or the furnishing of supplies or services. There shall be no deviation from this form without approval by the Administrator of General Services.

2. The full legal name and business address of the Principal shall be inserted in the space designated "Principal" on the face of this form. The bond shall be signed by an authorized person. Where such person is signing in a representative capacity (e.g., an attorney-in-fact), but is not a member of the firm, partnership, or joint venture, or an officer of the corporation involved, evidence of his authority must be furnished.

3. The penal sum of the bond may be expressed as a percentage of the bid price if desired. In such cases, a maximum dollar limitation may be stipulated (e.g., 20% of the bid price but the amount not to exceed _____ dollars).

4. (a) Corporations executing the bond as sureties must be among those appearing on the Treasury Department's list of approved sureties and must be acting within the limitations set forth therein. Where more than a single corporate surety is involved, their names and addresses (city and State) shall be inserted in the spaces (Surety A, Surety B, etc.) headed "CORPORATE SURETY(IES)", and in the space designated "SURETY(IES)" on the face of this form only the letter identification of the Sureties shall be inserted.

(b) Where individual sureties execute the bond, they shall be two or more responsible persons. A completed Affidavit of Individual Surety (Standard Form 28), for each individual surety, shall accompany the bond. Such sureties may be required to furnish additional substantiating information concerning their assets and financial capability as the Government may require.

5. Corporations executing the bond shall affix their corporate seals. Individuals shall execute the bond opposite the word "Seal"; and, if executed in Maine or New Hampshire, shall also affix an adhesive seal.

6. The name of each person signing this bid bond should be typed in the space provided.

U. S. GOVERNMENT PRINTING OFFICE : 1983 O - 394-813

Figure 3.4 (cont.)

PERFORMANCE BOND
(See Instructions on reverse)

	DATE BOND EXECUTED *(Must be same or later than date of contract)*

PRINCIPAL *(Legal name and business address)*

TYPE OF ORGANIZATION ("X" one)

☐ INDIVIDUAL   ☐ PARTNERSHIP

☐ JOINT VENTURE   ☐ CORPORATION

STATE OF INCORPORATION

SURETY(IES) *(Name(s) and business address(es))*

PENAL SUM OF BOND

MILLION(S)	THOUSAND(S)	HUNDRED(S)	CENTS

CONTRACT DATE	CONTRACT NO.

OBLIGATION:

We, the Principal and Surety(ies), are firmly bound to the United States of America (hereinafter called the Government) in the above penal sum. For payment of the penal sum, we bind ourselves, our heirs, executors, administrators, and successors, jointly and severally. However, where the Sureties are corporations acting as co-sureties, we, the Sureties, bind ourselves in such sum "jointly and severally" as well as "severally" only for the purpose of allowing a joint action or actions against any or all of us. For all other purposes, each Surety binds itself, jointly and severally with the Principal, for the payment of the sum shown opposite the name of the Surety. If no limit of liability is indicated, the limit of liability is the full amount of the penal sum.

CONDITIONS:

The Principal has entered into the contract identified above.

THEREFORE:

The above obligation is void if the Principal —

(a)(1) Performs and fulfills all the undertakings, covenants, terms, conditions, and agreements of the contract during the original term of the contract and any extensions thereof that are granted by the Government, with or without notice to the Surety(ies), and during the life of any guaranty required under the contract, and (2) perform and fulfills all the undertakings, covenants, terms conditions, and agreements of any and all duly authorized modifications of the contract that hereafter are made. Notice of those modifications to the Surety(ies) are waived.

(b) Pays to the Government the full amount of the taxes imposed by the Government, if the said contract is subject to the Miller Act, (40 U.S.C. 270a-270e), which are collected, deducted, or withheld from wages paid by the Principal in carrying out the construction contract with respect to which this bond is furnished.

WITNESS:

The Principal and Surety(ies) executed this performance bond and affixed their seals on the above date.

	PRINCIPAL		
Signature(s)	1. *(Seal)*	2. *(Seal)*	*Corporate Seal*
Name(s) & Title(s) *(Typed)*	1.	2.	

	INDIVIDUAL SURETY(IES)		
Signature(s)	1. *(Seal)*	2.	*(Seal)*
Name(s) *(Typed)*	1.	2.	

		CORPORATE SURETY(IES)		
SURETY A	Name & Address		STATE OF INC. LIABILITY LIMIT $	*Corporate Seal*
	Signature(s)	1.	2.	
	Name(s) & Title(s) *(Typed)*	1.	2.	

NSN 7540-01-152-8060
PREVIOUS EDITION USABLE

25-106

STANDARD FORM 25 (REV. 10-83)
Prescribed by GSA
FAR (48 CFR 53.228 (b))

Figure 3.5

			STATE OF INC.	LIABILITY LIMIT	
SURETY B	Name & Address			$	Corporate Seal
	Signature(s)	1.	2.		
	Name(s) & Title(s) (Typed)	1.	2.		
SURETY C	Name & Address		STATE OF INC.	LIABILITY LIMIT $	Corporate Seal
	Signature(s)	1.	2.		
	Name(s) & Title(s) (Typed)	1.	2.		
SURETY D	Name & Address		STATE OF INC.	LIABILITY LIMIT $	Corporate Seal
	Signature(s)	1.	2.		
	Name(s) & Title(s) (Typed)	1.	2.		
SURETY E	Name & Address		STATE OF INC.	LIABILITY LIMIT $	Corporate Seal
	Signature(s)	1.	2.		
	Name(s) & Title(s) (Typed)	1.	2.		
SURETY F	Name & Address		STATE OF INC.	LIABILITY LIMIT $	Corporate Seal
	Signature(s)	1.	2.		
	Name(s) & Title(s) (Typed)	1.	2.		
SURETY G	Name & Address		STATE OF INC.	LIABILITY LIMIT $	Corporate Seal
	Signature(s)	1.	2.		
	Name(s) & Title(s) (Typed)	1.	2.		

BOND PREMIUM ▶	RATE PER THOUSAND $	TOTAL $

INSTRUCTIONS

1. This form is authorized for use in connection with Government contracts. Any deviation from this form will require the written approval of the Administrator of General Services.

2. Insert the full legal name and business address of the Principal in the space designated "Principal" on the face of the form. An authorization person shall sign the bond. Any person signing in a representative capacity (e.g., an attorney-in-fact) must furnish evidence of authority if that representative is not a member of the firm, partnership, or joint venture, or an officer of the corporation involved.

3. (a) Corporations executing the bond as sureties must appear on the Department of the Treasury's list of approved sureties and must act within the limitation listed therein. Where more than one corporate surety is involved, their names and addresses shall appear in the spaces (Surety A, Surety B, etc.) headed "CORPORATE SURETY(IES)". In the space designated "SURETY(IES)" on the face of the form insert only the letter identification of the sureties.

(b) Where individual sureties are involved, two or more responsible persons shall execute the bond. A completed Affidavit of Individual Surety (Standard Form 28), for each individual surety, shall accompany the bond. The Government may require these sureties to furnish additional substantiating information concerning their financial capability.

4. Corporations executing the bond shall affix their corporate seals. Individuals shall execute the bond opposite the word "Corporate Seal"; and shall affix an adhesive seal if executed in Maine, New Hampshire, or any other jurisdiction requiring adhesive seals.

5. Type the name and title of each person signing this bond in the space provided.

STANDARD FORM 25 BACK (REV. 10-83)

☆ U.S. Government Printing Office: 1985—493-954/49112

Figure 3.5 (cont.)

PAYMENT BOND	DATE BOND EXECUTED (Must be same or later than date of contract)

PAYMENT BOND
(See Instructions on reverse)

PRINCIPAL *(Legal name and business address)*	TYPE OF ORGANIZATION ("X" one)

☐ INDIVIDUAL	☐ PARTNERSHIP
☐ JOINT VENTURE	☐ CORPORATION

STATE OF INCORPORATION

SURETY(IES) *(Name(s) and business address(es))*	PENAL SUM OF BOND			
	MILLION(S)	THOUSAND(S)	HUNDRED(S)	CENTS
	CONTRACT DATE	CONTRACT NO.		

OBLIGATION:

We, the Principal and Surety(ies), are firmly bound to the United States of America (hereinafter called the Government) in the above penal sum. For payment of the penal sum, we bind ourselves, our heirs, executors, administrators, and successors, jointly and severally. However, where the Sureties are corporations acting as co-sureties, we, the Sureties, bind ourselves in such sum "jointly and severally" as well as "severally" only for the purpose of allowing a joint action or actions against any or all of us. For all other purposes, each Surety binds itself, jointly and severally with the Principal, for the payment of the sum shown opposite the name of the Surety. If no limit of liability is indicated, the limit of liability is the full amount of the penal sum.

CONDITIONS:

The above obligation is void if the Principal promptly makes payment to all persons having a direct relationship with the Principal or a sub-contractor of the Principal for furnishing labor, material or both in the prosecution of the work provided for in the contract identified above, and any authorized modifications of the contract that subsequently are made. Notice of those modifications to the Surety(ies) are waived.

WITNESS:

The Principal and Surety(ies) executed this payment bond and affixed their seals on the above date.

	PRINCIPAL			
Signature(s)	1.	2.		
		(Seal)	(Seal)	*Corporate Seal*
Name(s) & Title(s) (Typed)	1.	2.		

	INDIVIDUAL SURETY(IES)		
Signature(s)	1.	2.	
		(Seal)	(Seal)
Name(s) (Typed)	1.	2.	

	CORPORATE SURETY(IES)	STATE OF INC.	LIABILITY LIMIT	
SURETY A	Name & Address		$	*Corporate Seal*
	Signature(s)	1.	2.	
	Name(s) & Title(s) (Typed)	1.	2.	

NSN 7540-01-152-8061
PREVIOUS EDITION USABLE

25-204

STANDARD FORM 25-A (REV. 10-83)
Prescribed by GSA
FAR (48 CFR 53.228(c))

Figure 3.6

	Name & Address		STATE OF INC.	LIABILITY LIMIT $	
SURETY B	Signature(s)	1.	2.		Corporate Seal
	Name(s) & Title(s) *(Typed)*	1.	2.		
SURETY C	Name & Address		STATE OF INC.	LIABILITY LIMIT $	Corporate Seal
	Signature(s)	1.	2.		
	Name(s) & Title(s) *(Typed)*	1.	2.		
SURETY D	Name & Address		STATE OF INC.	LIABILITY LIMIT $	Corporate Seal
	Signature(s)	1.	2.		
	Name(s) & Title(s) *(Typed)*	1.	2.		
SURETY E	Name & Address		STATE OF INC.	LIABILITY LIMIT $	Corporate Seal
	Signature(s)	1.	2.		
	Name(s) & Title(s) *(Typed)*	1.	2.		
SURETY F	Name & Address		STATE OF INC.	LIABILITY LIMIT $	Corporate Seal
	Signature(s)	1.	2.		
	Name(s) & Title(s) *(Typed)*	1.	2.		
SURETY G	Name & Address		STATE OF INC.	LIABILITY LIMIT $	Corporate Seal
	Signature(s)	1.	2.		
	Name(s) & Title(s) *(Typed)*	1.	2.		

INSTRUCTIONS

1. This form, for the protection of persons supplying labor and material, is used when a payment bond is required under the Act of August 24, 1935, 49 Stat. 793 (40 U.S.C. 270 a–270e). Any deviation from this form will require the written approval of the Administrator of General Services.

2. Insert the full legal name and business address of the Principal in the space designated "Principal" on the face of the form. An authorized person shall sign the bond. Any person signing in a representative capacity (e.g., an attorney-in-fact) must furnish evidence of authority if that representative is not a member of the firm, partnership, or joint venture, or an officer of the corporation involved.

3. (a) Corporations executing the bond as sureties must appear on the Department of the Treasury's list of approved sureties and must act within the limitation listed therein. Where more than one corporate surety is involved, their names and addresses shall appear in the spaces (Surety A, Surety B, etc.) headed "CORPORATE SURETY(IES)". In the space designated "SURETY(IES)" on the face of the form, insert only the letter identification of the sureties.

(b) Where individual sureties are involved, two or more responsible persons shall execute the bond. A completed Affidavit of Individual Surety (Standard Form 28), for each individual surety, shall accompany the bond. The Government may require these sureties to furnish additional substantiating information concerning their financial capability.

4. Corporations executing the bond shall affix their corporate seals. Individuals shall execute the bond opposite the word "Corporate Seal"; and shall affix an adhesive seal if executed in Maine, New Hampshire, or any other jurisdiction regarding adhesive seals.

5. Type the name and title of each person signing this bond in the space provided.

STANDARD FORM 25-A BACK (REV. 10-83)

GPO : 1984 O – 433–366

Figure 3.6 (cont.)

CONTRACT PRICING PROPOSAL COVER SHEET

| 1. SOLICITATION/CONTRACT/MODIFICATION NO. | FORM APPROVED OMB NO. 3090-0116 |

NOTE: This form is used in contract actions if submission of cost or pricing data is required. *(See FAR 15.804-6(b))*

| 2. NAME AND ADDRESS OF OFFEROR *(Include ZIP Code)* | 3A. NAME AND TITLE OF OFFEROR'S POINT OF CONTACT | 3B. TELEPHONE NO. |

4. TYPE OF CONTRACT ACTION *(Check)*

A. NEW CONTRACT	D. LETTER CONTRACT
B. CHANGE ORDER	E. UNPRICED ORDER
C. PRICE REVISION/ REDETERMINATION	F. OTHER *(Specify)*

5. TYPE OF CONTRACT *(Check)*

☐ FFP   ☐ CPFF   ☐ CPIF   ☐ CPAF

☐ FPI   ☐ OTHER *(Specify)*

6. PROPOSED COST *(A+B=C)*

| A. COST | B. PROFIT/FEE | C. TOTAL |
| $ | $ | $ |

7. PLACE(S) AND PERIOD(S) OF PERFORMANCE

8. List and reference the identification, quantity and total price proposed for each contract line item. A line item cost breakdown supporting this recap is required unless otherwise specified by the Contracting Officer. *(Continue on reverse, and then on plain paper, if necessary. Use same headings.)*

A. LINE ITEM NO.	B. IDENTIFICATION	C. QUANTITY	D. TOTAL PRICE	E. REF.

9. PROVIDE NAME, ADDRESS, AND TELEPHONE NUMBER FOR THE FOLLOWING *(If available)*

| A. CONTRACT ADMINISTRATION OFFICE | B. AUDIT OFFICE |
| | |

| 10. WILL YOU REQUIRE THE USE OF ANY GOVERNMENT PROPERTY IN THE PERFORMANCE OF THIS WORK? *(If "Yes," identify)* ☐ YES ☐ NO | 11A. DO YOU REQUIRE GOVERNMENT CONTRACT FINANCING TO PERFORM THIS PROPOSED CONTRACT? *(If "Yes," complete Item 11B)* ☐ YES ☐ NO | 11B. TYPE OF FINANCING *(√ one)* ☐ ADVANCE PAYMENTS ☐ PROGRESS PAYMENTS ☐ GUARANTEED LOANS |

| 12. HAVE YOU BEEN AWARDED ANY CONTRACTS OR SUBCONTRACTS FOR THE SAME OR SIMILAR ITEMS WITHIN THE PAST 3 YEARS? *(If "Yes," identify item(s), customer(s) and contract number(s))* ☐ YES ☐ NO | 13. IS THIS PROPOSAL CONSISTENT WITH YOUR ESTABLISHED ESTIMATING AND ACCOUNTING PRACTICES AND PROCEDURES AND FAR PART 31 COST PRINCIPLES? *(If "No," explain)* ☐ YES ☐ NO |

14. COST ACCOUNTING STANDARDS BOARD (CASB) DATA *(Public Law 91-379 as amended and FAR PART 30)*

| A. WILL THIS CONTRACT ACTION BE SUBJECT TO CASB REGULATIONS? *(If "No," explain in proposal)* ☐ YES ☐ NO | B. HAVE YOU SUBMITTED A CASB DISCLOSURE STATEMENT *(CASB DS-1 or 2)? (If "Yes," specify in proposal the office to which submitted and if determined to be adequate)* ☐ YES ☐ NO |
| C. HAVE YOU BEEN NOTIFIED THAT YOU ARE OR MAY BE IN NONCOMPLIANCE WITH YOUR DISCLOSURE STATEMENT OR COST ACCOUNTING STANDARDS? *(If "Yes," explain in proposal)* ☐ YES ☐ NO | D. IS ANY ASPECT OF THIS PROPOSAL INCONSISTENT WITH YOUR DISCLOSED PRACTICES OR APPLICABLE COST ACCOUNTING STANDARDS? *(If "Yes," explain in proposal)* ☐ YES ☐ NO |

This proposal is submitted in response to the RFP contract, modification, etc. in Item 1 and reflects our best estimates and/or actual costs as of this date.

| 15. NAME AND TITLE *(Type)* | 16. NAME OF FIRM |
| 17. SIGNATURE | 18. DATE OF SUBMISSION |

NSN 7540-01-142-9845

1411-101

STANDARD FORM 1411 (10-83)
Prescribed by GSA
FAR (48 CFR) 53.215-2(c)

U.S. GOVERNMENT PRINTING OFFICE : 1984 O - 437-443

Figure 3.7

Chapter Four
Managing and Administering the Contract

Managing and Administering the Contract

To effectively manage and administer a government construction contract, particular attention should naturally be paid to the areas that have the greatest influence on the project's success. The most important goals for the project are meeting the schedule, budget, and requirements of the plans and specifications. It is the purpose of this chapter to delve into these crucial areas. Included in the discussion are the levels of authority of government representatives, progress schedules, and submission of shop drawings.

Government Representatives

The role of the government's and contractor's representatives and the authority vested in these individuals are key issues in government contracting. When a contract is executed between a contractor and the federal government, the government representative who signs the contract is known as the *Contracting Officer*. Similarly, a corporate executive is usually assigned to execute the contract on behalf of the contractor. However, in the actual execution of the project on a day-to-day basis, neither the construction company executive nor the Contracting Officer are present at the job site. Furthermore, these two individuals are seldom involved in the administration that is required throughout the course of the contract. Both parties designate other representatives to handle the day-to-day functions of the job.

Designation of Government Representatives
The government's day-to-day representative may have several different designations, depending on the agency involved. He or she may be called the *Contracting Officer's Representative*, the *Officer in Charge of Construction*, the *Resident Officer in Charge of Construction*, or the *Resident Engineer*. At the beginning of the project, the government normally identifies in a formal letter both the Contracting Officer and the Contracting Officer's representative for day-to-day functions.

Levels of Authority
The letter identifying the government representative should include a designation of that individual's level of authority. This

information is generally expressed in terms of a dollar amount. For instance, the Corps of Engineers may designate by name a specific Contracting Officer's representative and specify that the limit of this individual's authority is $50,000. The Veterans Administration may designate a Resident Engineer as the representative on site and specify a level of authority of $5,000. The government representative can issue directives, field orders, or changes only up to the limit of the designated authority. This distinction is important to both the contractor and the government. All parties should be cognizant of the designated representative's identity and level of authority.

At the start of the project, the contractor should insure that all employees assigned to the project are fully aware of the appropriate government representative and that person's level of authority. If the contractor does not receive a letter from the Contracting Officer designating a representative and a level of authority, he should request this information as early as possible. The contractor, in turn, should inform the appropriate government representative(s) of the identity of his own authorized representative on the project site. The government needs to know who can act on behalf of the contractor.

Types of Authority

To avoid disputes and conflicts concerning the question of authority, it is important to understand not only the authority invested by dollar amount, but also these three additional types of authority:

1. Express authority
2. Implied authority
3. Apparent authority

Express Authority

Express authority is that which is directly granted to an individual in express terms and usually is given in writing. For example, the Contracting Officer writes to the contractor and designates an individual as the Contracting Officer's representative with a level of authority of $25,000.

Implied Authority

Implied authority is based on express authority and is the authority to direct any procedures necessary, usual, and proper to perform the work. For example, if the Contracting Officer specifies in a letter to the contractor that the representative on the site can approve extra work up to $25,000, implied in that authority is the fact that the representative can also direct extra work up to the limit of $25,000 or resolve questions relating to the project up to that amount of money.

Apparent Authority

Express authority and implied authority are relatively straightforward and easily understood. The third type of authority, apparent, is the area where problems usually arise. Apparent authority is that which an individual appears to possess by virtue of his actions and position. Problems occur when such an individual acts as if he has actual authority and causes another party to act in reliance on that apparent authority. Assume, for example, that the government is running a small project at an isolated base. The only government representative on the site is a construction inspector. During the course of the project, the inspector has issued various directives. These directives, for the most part, were relayed by the Contracting Officer's representative, through the inspector, to the contractor. The understanding of the contractor's personnel on the site is that the inspector can direct them to do extra work, and they do it accordingly. During the course of the project, several items of extra work are performed, the contractor submits change order requests for the extra work, and is paid. However, later on in the project, the inspector — without express or implied authority — directs the contractor to perform some extra work, which the contractor performs in the belief that the inspector has the authority to direct it. This time, when the contractor submits a request for a change order, the request is denied; the contractor is told that the government never issued that directive, nor did the inspector have the authority to issue it.

Misunderstanding of apparent authority can and should be avoided in order to head off unnecessary disputes over changes. In the above example, the contractor should have requested a directive from the authorized representative or the Contracting Officer, before performing the extra work. Requesting a directive from the authorized representative does not mean that the contractor will have an adversarial relationship with the inspector; all parties should understand that proper administration within the bounds of the contract documents requires the use of authorized directives.

The decisions of the Courts and the Boards have held that the government is not responsible or liable for a situation arising out of misunderstandings regarding apparent authority. (In contracts outside the federal government, however, a private owner may be found legally liable within the context of apparent authority.) Realistically, in most instances of apparent authority conflicts, the government usually resolves the situation, paying compensation to the contractor if extra work was indeed performed with an associated cost. However, there is no law or regulation that requires the government to pay a contractor for work that was improperly directed by an inspector (or other unauthorized individual) and arose out of an apparent authority situation.

Change Orders

Government representatives can direct a contractor to perform a change order only up to the amount authorized for that representative's level of authority. A representative whose limit is $10,000 cannot direct the contractor to perform a $75,000 change order, because that directive exceeds his level of authority. If a problem on a construction project requires the issuance of a change order the value of which is $75,000, the government's level of authority on the site must be at least $75,000.

Too often, improperly authorized extra work is performed for two reasons. First, the contractor does not provide a timely estimate of the cost for the change work and, therefore, the *value of the work* is not known. An assumption is made that the cost of the work will be within the representative's designated level of authority. The directive is then given and acted upon. The second cause of improperly authorized work is a lack of awareness of the government representative's *level of authority*. In this case, the contractor assumes that the government representative has the authority to direct the work. Both the contractor and the government should be aware of the level of authority of the representatives on the site and should be certain that if any extra work is directed by a government representative, that work is within the representative's level of authority.

If a government representative directs work that exceeds his level of authority, the contractor should not perform the work until a directive from the Contracting Officer (who has the appropriate level of authority) directs that amount of work. The government representative should not take offense if a contractor politely requests that the appropriate procedures be followed. The contractor is not questioning the representative's authority on the job, but rather is trying to administer the contract within the established procedures.

All parties should administer the project within the guidelines of the contract. On-site government personnel who are not properly authorized should not issue directives. By the same token, contractors should not follow directives that are not issued by the appropriate representative.

Oral and Written Directives

All parties who issue directives on a construction project should follow a simple rule: A directive given orally should be followed up with a very clear written version summarizing what is needed. A contractor who receives an oral directive should (before performing the extra work) follow up with written confirmation to the government representative. Such confirmation should specify that the work will be done per the oral directive issued on a certain date, and should indicate whether or not the work will involve extra cost. All too often, what one party says is not the same as what the other party hears. By committing an oral directive to writing, the facts of the situation are more clearly defined. This policy of following up an oral directive with a written document is not intended to "cover yourself" or foster a legalistic atmosphere on the project. Its purpose is simply to clarify the issue for all parties concerned.

On occasion, a government representative may issue oral directives to a contractor, but refuse to give the contractor written verification. It is in the best interest of the contractor to insist on a written directive. If, for some reason, the contractor cannot obtain the directive in writing, he should follow up with written clarification of this fact. There is no legitimate reason why a government representative should not follow up an oral directive in writing.

Agency Procedures and Policies

A contractor working with the federal government on construction contracts must recognize that each agency has different procedures and policies. At the start of a construction project, the contractor should make it a point to become familiar with relevant procedures and policies, and should discuss them with representatives of the government agency prior to beginning the work. The *pre-construction conference* provides an ideal opportunity for this discussion. All too often, needless paperwork arises and problems are not resolved because one party or the other is not following the established procedures. Both parties, including the construction staff, must know and follow the procedures during the administration of the project.

Because each agency is different within the federal government, the procedures that the contractor followed on past projects with the Corps of Engineers, for example, may not necessarily be the same that will be followed on a new project with the Veterans Administration. Some of the differences among the agencies are briefly discussed in Chapter 12.

Progress Schedules

All federal construction projects require the submission of some form of a progress schedule. The requirements for this schedule vary tremendously from agency to agency and even within one agency. Some projects require a simple bar chart for scheduling work, while the Veterans Administration, for example, usually requires a detailed cost-loaded and resource-loaded Critical Path Method (CPM) schedule. Examples of these two types of schedules are shown in Figures 4.1 and 4.2.

The contractor must realize that submitting and updating a progress schedule is an absolute necessity if the government is to properly administer the construction project. A progress schedule is crucial to the proper administration of the contractor's business as well. Both parties — and the project itself — benefit tremendously if a detailed schedule for the project is used. Some of the biggest disputes that occur on construction projects are concerned with delays. Consequently, proper control of time on the project is bound to improve the prospects for everyone's success.

The schedule provides details of the activities that are involved in constructing a job, the interrelationship and duration of those activities, and, if possible, the resources involved in accomplishing the activities. Unfortunately, most government projects require only the submission of a bar chart. In many cases, the bar chart depicts too few activities to properly assess the progress of the job in terms of time. Regardless of the government's requirements, it is strongly recommended that all contractors utilize the Critical Path Method (CPM) for scheduling for construction projects.

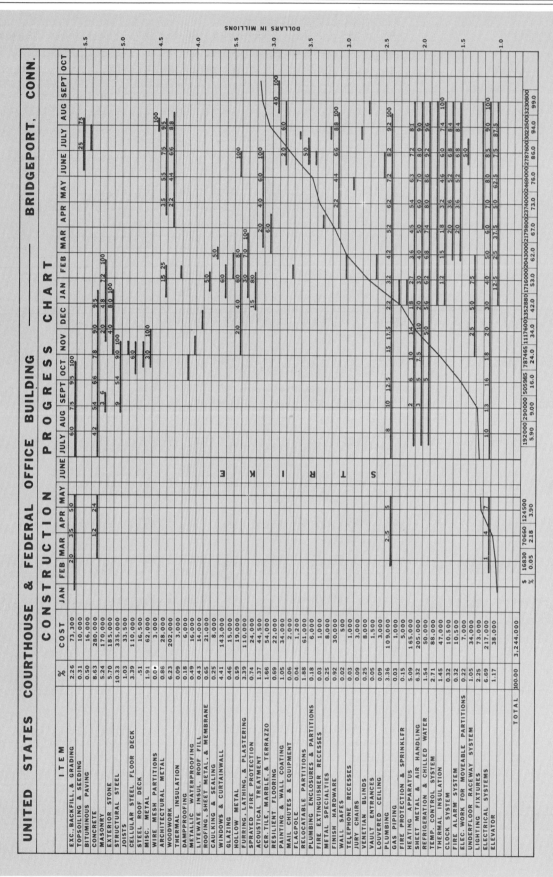

Figure 4.1   **Sample Bar Chart**

62

Critical Path Method

The Critical Path Method (CPM) for scheduling construction projects has been in use since the late 1950's. Many people in the construction business do not use this method because they feel it is too difficult, too time consuming, and consequently, too expensive. In reality, CPM is not difficult to use, and offers tremendous advantages. In the end, a good schedule is worth the investment if it allows the contractor to properly control time.

While the CPM Method is recommended for *all* projects, the following simple guideline can be used to determine when it is absolutely necessary. A contractor can manage time *without* a CPM schedule if he can mentally retain all of the activities of the project, together with their interrelationships. If this is the case, the contractor can effectively manage the job using only a bar chart. It is possible to use a bar chart for a complex project, but the chart would have to be extremely detailed. This approach, using a complex bar chart, is effectively the same as that used for a CPM Schedule. The key is to have a reasonably detailed schedule showing the interrelationships among activities. A schedule with these features should be a useful tool.

Updating the Schedule

Once a project schedule has been submitted and approved, it can be used by both parties to monitor the progress of the job. The schedule must be updated on a regular basis. The intervals at which updates are made tend to vary with the duration of the project. For most projects with a duration greater than six

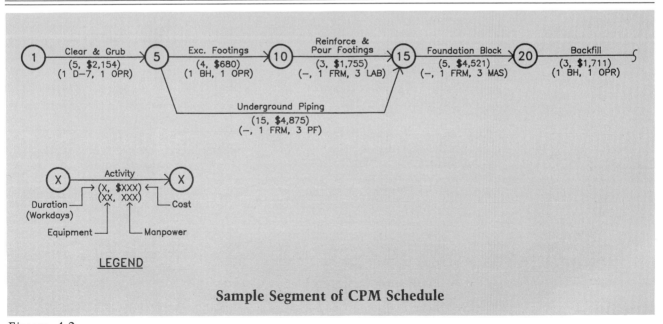

Sample Segment of CPM Schedule

Figure 4.2

months, monthly updating is adequate, though it may, in some cases, be more frequent. Seldom, if ever, should updates be less frequent than once a month.

Although it is the contractor's responsibility to update the schedule, the government should also be involved in this process. Government representatives should be reviewing the updates to ensure that they are accurate and should be discussing with the contractor (during the schedule review meetings or progress meetings) the progress of the project relative to the schedule and the overall completion date.

The requirement for submitting a progress schedule and updates may be the most significant submittal requirement in the entire federal contract, and deserves the careful attention of both parties. The various government agencies have differing requirements for administering the schedule. Figure 4.3 is a sample specification from a project which was constructed for the Veterans Administration and is shown at the end of this chapter. Several points are worthy of note on this specification. First, the Veterans Administration places a high level of importance on the CPM schedule for the project. Consequently, this agency requires an independent scheduling professional to prepare and update the schedule. Second, the schedule is the basis for payments to the contractor throughout the project. It is also the base line and the vehicle used for granting time extensions for the project. Third, the Veterans Administration does the monthly updating of the schedule based on the progress reported by the contractor. Fourth, the schedule is not only cost-loaded but also manpower-loaded. Fifth, all change orders must include schedule information. Clearly, the Veterans Administration requires a detailed, comprehensive schedule of the project. This approach is completely justified since a poorly scheduled project invites more problems for all parties.

The Veterans Administration's practice of being actively involved in the scheduling and then updating is a sound one. While more federal agencies are requiring in their specifications the submission of a CPM schedule, this trend has not, in many cases, realistically improved the scheduling on the project. Merely requiring a CPM schedule does not assure that it will be of any value. In fact, far too many contractors view a contract specification for a CPM schedule as just another headache. Consequently, they may do only the absolute minimum to satisfy the specification, and may not end up with a useful management tool. That is one of the reasons the Veterans Administration is so actively involved in the scheduling of its projects.

It is the authors' opinion that all federal agencies should be more involved in the scheduling for a project. Figure 4.4 (shown at the end of the chapter) is a draft scheduling specification that has been suggested by the authors to some federal agencies for use in their contracts. While not as detailed as the preceding Veteran's Administration specification, it does give the agency far more control over the quality of the schedule and updates.

Submission of Shop Drawings

In addition to schedules, many other types of submissions are required during the course of the project. The type of submission that the contractor must prepare most frequently involves shop drawings. Most federal contracts have specific clauses that address the requirement for the submission of shop drawings. Such clauses generally point out that no work can be performed until the shop drawing submittal has been approved. They may also note that a contractor who performs work prior to the approval of the submission is doing that work at risk. If the submittals or the shop drawings are disapproved or altered by the government and the contractor has already performed the work, the contractor may have to redo that work at his own expense.

In the general context of submittals on a construction project, the following guidelines should be followed by both the contractor and the government.

1. The contractor should prepare the submittals in detail, and should insure that each fulfills the requirements of the contract documents. Careful preparation prevents the problem of submittals returned marked, "rejected — resubmit," due to insufficient detail.

2. If the contractor is submitting items prepared by subcontractors or suppliers, he is obligated to first review these documents for compliance with the contract documents before submitting them to the government representative. Unfortunately, in too many cases, the general contractor merely "rubber stamps" submissions from subcontractors or suppliers without really reviewing them in the context of the contract requirements. Again, this "short cut" may lead to an unnecessary waste of time in the form of rejections and resubmittals.

3. If the contractor is submitting an item that deviates from the contract documents in any respect, that deviation should be clearly noted — both on the submission and on the submittal transmission or submittal letter.

4. The contractor should ensure that all submittals are presented in a timely fashion and in accordance with the project schedule so as not to delay the work.

5. In most federal contracts, the contractor is required to prepare a *submittal log*. At the beginning of the project, the log shows a schedule with a breakdown of the submittals that will be supplied. The contractor must then update the submittal log to reflect when the items are actually submitted and when they are returned. It is important to both parties that this submittal log be maintained accurately and on a regular basis throughout the project. When disputes arise over delays, either to the project or to specific items, the main source of reference to resolve a problem is often the submittal log and submittal information.

6. Government representatives should review all submittals in a timely fashion. Unfortunately, in some cases, the exact time allowed for this review is not specified. Instead the phrase, "within a reasonable time," is used. If possible,

government representatives should specify a set amount of time in terms of calendar days or working days and then ensure that the agency fulfills that obligation to review the submissions within that time frame.

7. The government should apply a reasonable standard in reviewing submittals. There are occasions where, after reviewing submittals, the government returns them *not approved* merely because some dimensions were not broken out on the drawings, even though those dimensions could have been deduced simply by consulting the drawings.

Government representatives should also avoid using submittals or shop drawings as a vehicle for making changes. In some instances, the government may recognize — by virtue of the shop drawing submission — that there will be a problem in building the project as designed. Their representatives may try to overcome the problem by making modifications to the shop drawings. By specifying changes on a submittal, the government representative is asking the contractor to perform extra work or a change that is not specified in the contract.

If an outside design firm is used for review of the shop drawings, the government should ensure that this firm's representatives comply with the time requirements in the review and return of submittals.

A contractor who submits information to the government or requests information from the government, should specify a time requirement for the return of that submittal or information. In turn, the government should expedite those requests within the specified time requirements, particularly requests for information where clarifications are needed in order for the contractor to continue work on specific areas of the project.

Record Keeping

All projects require a certain level of record keeping and documentation. Unfortunately, many people feel that this is an unnecessary and time-consuming requirement. On the contrary, proper documentation on a construction project is extremely important and absolutely necessary, because it provides a continuous record of what occurs on the job.

Proper documentation is required for many reasons. Among the most prominent are: having accurate record drawings of the project in case future construction is performed; for resolving disputes that may arise over what work was directed; and for documenting costs for extra work that may have been performed.

The importance of proper documentation cannot be stressed enough. All parties should write more rather than less.

Good project documentation would allow someone new to take over responsibility for a project in progress, finding from the records what has transpired in terms of progress, work, and changes, and being able to effectively administer the remaining work with no additional information.

Detailed and specific record keeping practices established at the beginning of a project become a routine and are not so readily viewed as an inconvenience.

The guidelines noted above are fairly general. If they are followed religiously by both parties, the administration of the project runs far more smoothly and complements the orderly and efficient execution of the project.

Section 01311

Network Analysis System

Part I - GENERAL:

1.1 DESCRIPTION:

A. The Contractor shall develop a Network Analysis System (NAS) plan and schedule demonstrating fulfillment of the contract requirements, shall keep the network up to date in accordance with the requirements of this section and shall utilize the plan for scheduling, coordinating and monitoring work under this contract (including all activities of subcontractors, equipment vendors and suppliers). Conventional Critical Path Method (CPM) (I-J) technique will be utilized to satisfy both time and cost applications.

B. Use the principles and definitions of the terms in the Associated General Contractors of America (AGCA) publication, "The Use of CPM in Construction, A Manual for General Contractors and the Construction Industry," Copyright 1976, except the provisions specified in this section shall govern.

1.2 CONTRACTOR'S REPRESENTATIVE:

A. The Contractor shall designate an authorized representative in the firm who will be responsible for the preparation of the network diagram, review and report progress of the project with and to the Contracting Officer's representative. The Contractor's representative shall have direct project control and complete authority to act on behalf of the Contractor in fulfilling the requirements of this specification section and such authority shall not be interrupted throughout the duration of the project.

1.3 CONTRACTORS'S CONSULTANT:

A. To assist in the preparation of the project plan, arrow diagram, and tape, the Contractor shall engage an independent CPM consultant who is skilled in the time and cost application of activity on arrow (I-J) network techniques for construction projects, at no additional cost to the Government. This consultant shall not have any financial or business ties to the Contractor, and shall not be an affiliate or subsidiary company of the Contractor, and shall not be employed by an affiliate or subsidiary company of the Contractor.

-16-

Sample VA Specification

Figure 4.3

68

B.   Prior to engaging a consultant, and within ten calendar days after award of the contract, the Contractor shall submit to the Contracting Officer:

1.   The name and address of the proposed consultant.

2.   Sufficient information to show that the proposed consultant has the qualifications to meet the requirements specified in the preceding paragraph.

3.   A list of prior construction projects, along with selected activity on arrow (I-J) network on current projects which the proposed consultant has performed. These network samples must show complete project planning for a project of similar size and scope as covered under this contract.

C.   The Contract Officer has the right to approve or disapprove employment of the proposed consultant, and will notify the Contractor of the VA decision within seven calendar days from receipt of information. In case of disapproval, the Contractor shall resubmit another consultant within ten calendar days for renewed consideration. The Contractor must have their CPM consultant approved prior to submitting any diagram.

1.4 COMPUTER-PRODUCED SCHEDULES:

A.   The Veterans Administration (VA) will provide to the Contractor monthly computer processing of all computer-produced time/cost schedules and reports as a result of the monthly project updates. This computer service will include up to five copies of any five reports currently available on the VACPM computer program. The VA will only provide computer processing and associated reports for the monthly project updates.

B.   The VA will produce the five requested reports from the approved, cost-loaded, interim arrow diagram or the completed project arrow diagram. The requested reports will be produced upon receipt of the completed Look-Ahead Report. The VA assumes responsibility for the correctness and timeliness of computer-produced reports. The Contractor is responsible for the accurate and timely submittal of the updated Look-Ahead Report and all CPM data necessary to produce the computer reports and payment request that are specified.

C.   The Contractor shall report errors in computer-produced reports to the Contracting Officer's representative within seven calendar days from Contractor's receipt of reports. The Contracting Officer will reprocess the

-17-

Figure 4.3 (cont.)

computer-produced reports to correct update errors only if the errors substantially affect the payment and schedule for the project.

1.5 INTERIM ARROW DIAGRAM SUBMITTAL:

A. Within 21 calendar days after receipt of Notice to Proceed, the Contractor shall submit for the Contracting Officer's review, five blue line copies of an Interim Arrow Diagram on sheets of 28 inch by 42 inch paper a magnetic tape(s), and five copies of a computer-produced I-J schedule. The I-J computer-produced schedule shall meet all contractual requirements such as contract duration, phases, and phasing restraints. The Interim Arrow Diagram shall cover the following project phases and activities:

1. Procurement - Submittals, approvals, fabrication and delivery of all key and long lead time procurement activities.

2. The activities to be accomplished during the first 120 work days of the project.

3. Summary activities which are necessary (not included under paragraph above) to properly show:

   a. The approach to scheduling the remaining work areas or phases of the project. The work for each phase or area must be represented by at least one (summary) activity so that the work cumulatively shows the entire project schedule.

   b. Approximate cost and duration for each summary activity which is the Contractor's best estimate for all the work represented.

   c. Realistic delivery dates for all procurement activities required and specified.

4. In addition to the Interim Arrow Diagram, the Contractor shall submit five copies of a computer-produced I-J schedule showing project duration, phase completion dates and activity cost. Each activity on the computer-produced schedule shall contain as a minimum, but not limited to, I-J nodes, duration, trade, area, description, budget amount, early start date, early finish date, late start date, late finish date, and total float. The Contractor shall submit a magnetic tape for the Interim Diagram

-18-

Figure 4.3 (cont.)

submission, as specified under Article ARROW DIAGRAM
REQUIREMENTS, PARAGRAPH MAGNETIC TAPE REQUIREMENTS.

B.   The Interim Diagram shall describe the activities to be
     accomplished and their interdependencies subject to all
     requirements specified, where appropriate. All work
     activities, other than procurement activities, shall be cost
     loaded as specified and is the basis for partial payment
     during the beginning months of the contract, while the
     complete working arrow diagram is being developed and
     approved. Interim diagram shall not be used for time
     extension analysis. All CPM data supporting any time
     extension request, in accordance with Article ADJUSTMENT OF
     CONTRACT COMPLETION, WILL BE DERIVED FROM THE APPROVED FINAL
     ARROW DIAGRAM.

C.   Within 21 calendar days of receipt by the Contracting
     Officer of the Interim Arrow Diagram, the Contracting
     Officer shall notify the Contractor concerning approval or
     disapproval of the Interim Arrow Diagram. In the event of
     disapproval, The Contractor shall resubmit, within 14
     calendar days, five blue line copies of the revised arrow
     diagram, five copies of the revised computer produced I-J
     schedule, and a revised magnetic tape in accordance with any
     agreements reached as a result of the Contracting Officer's
     review.

1.6 THE COMPLETE PROJECT ARROW DIAGRAM SUBMITTAL:

A.   Within 90 calendar days after receipt of Notice to Proceed,
     the Contractor shall submit for the Contracting Officer's
     review five blue line copies of the complete arrow diagram
     on sheets 28 inches by 42 inches, and magnetic tape(s) as
     specified. The submittal shall also include five copies of a
     computer-produced I-J schedule showing project duration;
     phase completion dates; all dummies; and other data,
     including activity cost. Each activity on the
     computer-produced schedule shall contain as a minimum, but
     not limited to, I-J nodes, duration, trade, area,
     description, budget amount, early start date, early finish
     date, late start date, late finish date and total float. The
     complete working arrow diagram shall reflect the
     Contractor's approach to scheduling the complete project,
     taking into account the accuracy of the logic and the
     experience gained from the interim diagram. The final
     diagram in its original form shall contain no contract
     changes or delays which may have been incurred during the
     interim diagram period. These changes/delays shall be
     entered at the first update after the final diagram has been
     approved. The Contractor should provide their request/time

-19-

Figure 4.3 (cont.)

extension analysis for contract time as a result of these contract changes/delays after this update and in accordance with Article, ADJUSTMENT OF CONTRACT COMPLETION.

B. Within 30 calendar days after receipt of the complete project arrow diagram, the Contracting Officer or his representative will do one or both of the following:

1. Notify the Contractor concerning his actions, opinions, and objections.

2. A meeting with the Contractor at or near the job site for joint review, correction, or adjustment of the proposed plan will be scheduled if required. Within 14 calendar days after the joint review, the Contractor shall revise and shall submit five blue line copies of the revised arrow diagram, five copies of the revised computer-produced (I-J) schedule, and a revised magnetic tape to the Contracting Officer. The resubmission will be reviewed by the Contracting Officer and, if found to be as previously agreed upon, will be approved.

C. The VA will process and return approved arrow diagram and computer reports as specified to the Contractor. The approved arrow diagram and the computer-produced schedule(s) generated therefrom shall constitute the project work schedule until subsequently revised in accordance with requirements of this section.

D. The Complete Project Arrow Diagram will contain, including dummies, no less than 600 activities and no more than 1200 activities.

1.7 ACTIVITY COST DATA:

A. The Contractor shall cost load all work activities except procurement activities. The cumulative amount of all cost loaded work activities shall equal the total contract price. Prorate overhead, profit, and general conditions on all activities for the entire project length. The VA will generate from this information cash flow curves indicating graphically the total percentages of activity dollar value scheduled to be in place on early finish, late finish, and 50 percent float dates. These cash flow cures will be used by the Contracting Officer to assist him in determining approval or disapproval. The contractor shall revise and resubmit in accordance with Article, INTERIM ARROW DIAGRAM SUBMITTAL and THE COMPLETE ARROW DIAGRAM SUBMITTAL.

-20-

Figure 4.3 (cont.)

B. The Contractor shall cost load activities for test, balance and adjust various systems in accordance with the provisions in the General Conditions, Article, PAYMENT UNDER FIXED-PRICE CONSTRUCTION CONTRACTS 9VA SUPPLEMENTAL CONDITIONS.

C. In accordance with Article PERFORMANCE OF WORK BY THE CONTRACTOR (VAAR 852.236) in the Section, GENERAL CONDITIONS, the Contractor shall submit, simultaneously with the cost per activity of the construction schedule required by this Section, a responsibility code for all activities (referred to as "branches" in the GENERAL CONDITIONS) of the network for which the Contractor's forces will perform the work.

1.8 ARROW DIAGRAM REQUIREMENTS:

A. Show on the arrow diagram the sequence and interdependence of activities required for complete performance of all items of work. In preparing the arrow diagram, the contractor shall:

1. Exercise sufficient care to produce a clear, legible and accurate diagram including all copies that refer to the drawing, CPM-1 (Sample CPM Network). Group activities related to specific physical areas of the project, on the diagram, for ease of understanding and simplification. Provide a key plan on each diagram sheet showing the project area associated with the activities shown on that sheet.

2. Show the following on each work activity:

a. I and J (beginning and ending event number, respectively).

b. Concise description of the work represented by the activity (29 characters or less including spaces).

c. Performance responsibility or trade code (five characters or less): GEN, MECH, ELEC, CARP, PLAST, or other acceptable abbreviations.

d. Duration (in work days).

e. Cost (in accordance with Article, ACTIVITY COST DATE of this section and less than $9,999,999 per activity).

f. Work location on area cost (five characters or less), descriptive of the area involved.

-21-

Figure 4.3 (cont.)

g.   Manpower required (average number of men per day).

h.   CPM legend format shown on the drawing, CPM-1 (Sample CPM Network) is mandatory and shall be followed in preparing interim and final arrow diagrams.

3.   Show such activities as:

a.   Contractor's time required for submittal of shop drawings, templates, fabrication, delivery and similar pre-construction work.

b.   Contracting Officer's and Architect-Engineer's review and approval of shop drawings, equipment schedules, samples, template or similar items.

c.   Interruption of VA Medical Center utilities, delivery of Government furnished equipment, project phasing and any other specification requirements.

d.   Test, balance and adjust various systems and pieces of equipment.

4.   Show not only the activities for actual construction work for each trade category of the project, but also include trade dummies to indicate the movement of trades from one area, floor, or building, to another area, floor, or building, for at least five trades who are performing major work under this contract.

5.   Break up the work into activities of a duration no longer than 20 work days each, except as to non-construction activities i.e., (procurement of materials, delivery of equipment, concrete and asphalt curing) and any other activities for which the Contracting Officer may approve the showing of longer duration. The duration for VA approval of any required submittal, shop drawing, or other submittals shall not be less than 20 work days. The construction time as determined by the CPM schedule from early start to late finish for any subphase, phase or the entire project shall not exceed the contract time(s) specified or shown.

6.   Describe work activities clearly, so the work is readily identifiable for assessment of completion. Activities labeled "start," "continue," or

-22-

Figure 4.3 (cont.)

"completion," are not specified and will not be allowed. Lead and lag time activities will be acceptable.

7. Uniquely number each activity with event numbers ranging from 1 to 29900 only. The diagram should be generally numbered in sequence, left to right, top to bottom, and omitting numbers ending in 3, 6, and 9 with J node always being greater than I node.

B. Submit the following arrow diagram supporting data in addition to the arrow diagram, I-J schedule, and magnetic tape. Failure of the Contractor to include this data will delay the review of the submittal until the Contracting Officer is in receipt of the missing data:

1. The proposed number of working days per week.

2. The holidays to be observed during the life of the contract (by day, month, and year).

3. The planned number of shifts per day.

4. The number of hours per shift.

5. The major construction equipment to be used on the site.

C. To the extent that the arrow diagram or any revised arrow diagram shows anything not jointly agreed upon, it shall not be deemed to have been approved by the Contracting Officer. Failure to include any element of work required for the performance of this contract shall not excuse the contractor from completing all work required within any applicable completion date of each phase regardless of the Contracting Officer's approval of the arrow diagram.

D. Magnetic Tape Requirements: Submit to the VA a tape containing the data required to produce an I-J computer-produced schedule, reflecting all the activities of the interim diagram and complete project arrow diagram being submitted. Produce the magnetic tape in the format specified and shown below:

-23-

Figure 4.3 (cont.)

1. Work Activity Record:

COLUMNS	FIELD NAME	REMARK
1-6	Blank	Filled with spaces
7-11	I Node	Right justify, left zero fill, numeric
12-16	J Node	Right justify, left zero fill, numeric
17-21	Blank	Fill with spaces
22-24	Duration	Right justify, left zero fill, numeric
25-29	Trade or Responsibility	Left justify, right space fill, alpha-numeric
30-34	Area	Left justify, right space fill, alpha-numeric
35-37	Blank	Fill with spaces
38-72	Description	Left justify, right space fill, alpha-numeric
73-79	Blank	Fill with spaces
80	Transaction Code	Insert Character "1"

2. Restraint or Dummy Activity Card:

COLUMNS	FIELD NAME	REMARK
1-6	Blank	Fill with spaces
7-11	I Node	Right justify, left zero fill, numeric
12-16	J Node	right justify, left zero fill, numeric
17-37	Blank	Fill with spaces
38	Restraint or Dummy Activity	(Less - than sign)
39-79	Blank	Fill with spaces
90	Transaction Code	Insert character "1"

3. Activity Budget Record:

COLUMNS	FIELD NAME	REMARK
1-6	Blank	Fill with spaces
7-11	I Node	Right justify, left zero fill, numeric
12-16	J Node	Right justify, left zero fill, numeric
17-18	Blank	Fill with spaces
19-26	Budget Amt.	[9 (6) V99] numeric, right justify (allowing positions 25 and 26 cents), left zero fill dollars and zero fill cents if not available

-24-

Figure 4.3 (cont.)

| 27-79 | Blank | Fill with spaces |
| 80 | Transaction Code | Insert character "5" |

4. Activity Manpower Record:

COLUMNS	FIELD NAME	REMARK
1-6	Blank	Fill with spaces
7-11	I Node	Right justify, left zero fill, numeric
12-16	J Node	Right justify, left zero fill, numeric
17-76	Blank	Fill with spaces
77-79	Manpower	Numeric, right justify, left zero fill
80	Transaction Code	Insert Character "4"

E.   Magnetic Tape Requirements

Label: Unlabeled
Density: 9 track; 1600 BPI
Record Length: 80 characters
Block Size: 5760 characters (72 records)
Character Set: EBCDCIC or ASCII Standard 7-bit code

The magnetic tape will be returned to the Contractor after the data has run on the VA CPM system.

1.9 PAYMENT TO THE CONTRACTOR:

A.   The monthly submission of the Veterans Administration "Look-Ahead Report" showing updated activities and cost data in accordance with the provisions of the following Payment and Progress Reporting is the basis upon which progress payments will be made pursuant to Article, PAYMENT UNDER FIXED-PRICE CONSTRUCTION CONTRACTS (VAAR 852.236-83) of Section GENERAL CONDITIONS. The Contractor is entitled to progress payment upon approval of estimates as determined from the currently approved updated computer-produced calendar-dated schedule unless, in a special situation, the Contracting Officer permits an exception to this requirement.

B.   When the Contractor fails or refuses to furnish the information and CPM Data which, in the sole judgement of the contracting Officer, is necessary for processing the computer produced calendar-dated schedules, the contractor shall not be deemed to have provided an estimate upon which progress payment may be made.

-25-

Figure 4.3 (cont.)

1.10 PAYMENT AND PROGRESS REPORTING:

A.   Monthly job site progress meetings shall be held on dates mutually agreed to by the Contracting Officer (or Contracting Officer's representative) and the Contractor. Contractor and CPM consultant will be required to attend all monthly progress meetings. Presence of Subcontractors during progress meeting is optional unless required by the Contracting Officer (or Contracting Officer's representative). The Contractor shall complete their copy of the "Look-Ahead Report" and all other data required by this Section shall be accurately filled in and completed prior to the monthly progress meeting. The Contractor shall provide this information to the Contracting Officer or the VA representative in completed form three work days in advance of the progress meeting. Job Progress will be reviewed to verify:

1.   Actual finish dates for completed activities.

2.   Remaining duration required to complete each activity started, or scheduled to start, but not completed.

3.   Logic, time, and cost data for change orders, and supplemental agreements that agree to be incorporated into the arrow diagram and computer-produced schedules. Changes in activity sequence and durations which have been made pursuant to the provisions of following Article, ADJUSTMENT OF CONTRACT COMPLETION.

4.   Percentage for completed and partially completed activities.

5.   Logic and duration revisions required by this section of the specifications.

B.   The Contractor shall submit a narrative report as a part of his monthly review and update in a form agreed upon by the Contractor and the Contracting Officer. The narrative report shall include a description of problem areas, current and anticipated delaying factors and their estimated impact of performance of other activities and completion dates, and an explanation of corrective action taken or proposed. This report is in addition to the daily reports pursuant to the provisions of Article, DAILY REPORT OF WORKER AND MATERIAL in the GENERAL CONDITIONS.

-26-

Figure 4.3 (cont.)

C. After completion of the joint review and the Contracting Officer's approval of all entries, the VA will generate an updated computer-produced, calendar-dated schedule and supply the Contractor with reports in accordance with the Article, COMPUTER PRODUCED SCHEDULES, specified.

D. After each monthly update, the Contractor shall submit to the Contracting Officer blue line copies of a revised complete arrow diagram showing all completed and partially completed activities, contract changes and logic changes made on the subject update. Monthly updates using the interim arrow diagram are exempted from this requirement.

1.11 RESPONSIBILITY FOR COMPLETION:

A. Whenever it becomes apparent from the current monthly progress review meeting or the monthly computer-produced, calendar-dated schedule that phasing or contract completion dates will not be met, the Contractor shall execute some or all of the following remedial actions:

1. Increase construction manpower in such quantities and crafts as necessary to eliminate the backlog work.

2. Increase the number of working hours per shift, shifts per working day, working days per week, the amount of construction equipment, or any combination of the foregoing to eliminate the backlog of work.

3. Reschedule the work in conformance with the specification requirements.

B. Prior to proceeding with any of the above actions, the Contractor shall notify and obtain approval from the Contracting Officer for the proposed schedule changes. If such actions are approved, the CPM revisions shall be incorporated by the Contractor into the arrow diagram before the next update, at no additional cost to the Government.

1.12 CHANGES TO ARROW DIAGRAM AND SCHEDULE:

A. Within 30 calendar days after receipt of any computer-produced schedule, the Contractor will submit a revised arrow diagram and a (I-J) list of any activity changes for any of the following reasons:

1. Delay in completion of any activity or group of activities, indicate an extension of the project completion by 20 working days or 10 percent of the

-27-

Figure 4.3 (cont.)

remaining project duration, whichever is less. Such delays which may be involved with contract changes, strikes, unusual weather, and other delays will not relieve the Contractor from the requirements specified unless the conditions are shown on the CPM as the direct cause for delaying the project beyond the acceptable limits.

    2.   Delays in submittals, deliveries, or work stoppage are encountered which make replanning or rescheduling of the work necessary.

    3.   The schedule does not represent the actual prosecution and progress of the project.

    4.   Activity costs are revised as the result of contract modifications.

B.   CPM revisions made under this paragraph which affect the previously approved computer-produced schedules for Government furnished equipment, vacating of areas by the VA Medical Center, contract phase(s) and subphase(s), utilities furnished by the Government to the Contractor, or any other previously contracted item must be furnished in writing to the Contracting Officer for approval.

C.   Contracting Officer's approval for the revised arrow diagram and all relevant data is contingent upon compliance with all other paragraphs of this section and any other previous agreements by the Contracting Officer or the VA representative.

D.   The cost of revisions to the arrow diagram resulting from contract changes will be included in the proposal for changes in work as specified in Article, CONTRACT CHANGES of the GENERAL CONDITIONS, and will be based on the complexity of the revision or contract change, expended in analyzing the change, and the total cost of the change.

E.   The cost of revisions to the arrow diagram not resulting from contract changes is the responsibility of the Contractor.

1.13 ADJUSTMENT OF CONTRACT COMPLETION:

A.   The contract completion time will be adjusted only for causes specified in the contract. Request for any extension of the contract completion date by the contractor shall be supported with a justification, CPM data and supporting evidence as the Contracting Officer

-28-

Figure 4.3 (cont.)

may deem necessary for determination as to whether or not the Contractor is entitled to an extension of time under the provisions of the contract. Submission of proof based on revised activity logic durations and costs is obligatory to any approvals. The schedule must clearly display that the schedule has used, in full, all the float time available for the work involved in this request. The Contracting Officer's determination as to the total number of days of contract extension will be based upon the current computer-produced, calendar-dated schedule for the time period in question and all other relevant information. Actual delays in activities which, according to the computer-produced, calendar-dated schedule, do not affect the extended and predicated contract completion dates shown by the critical path in the network, will not be the basis for a change to the contract completion date. The Contracting Officer will, within a reasonable time after receipt of such justification and supporting evidence, review the facts and advise the Contractor in writing of the Contracting Officer's decision.

B.   The Contractor shall submit each request for a change in the contract completion date to the Contracting Officer in accordance with the provisions specified under Article, CONTRACT CHANGES, in the Section, GENERAL CONDITIONS. The Contractor shall include, as part of each change order proposal, a sketch showing all CPM logic revisions, duration changes, and cost changes, for work in question and its relationship to other activities on the approved arrow diagram.

-29-

Figure 4.3 (cont.)

DRAFT

SCHEDULING SPECIFICATION

The construction of this project will be planned and recorded with a conventional Critical Path Method (CPM) schedule. The schedule shall be sued for coordination, monitoring, and payment of all work under the contract including all activity of subcontractors, vendors, and suppliers.

The CONTRACTOR is responsible for preparing the initial schedule in the form of an activity on arrow diagram. The GOVERNMENT will provide a scheduling expert to work with the CONTRACTOR in preparing the initial schedule. The GOVERNMENT is responsible for providing computer processing of the scheduling data provided by the CONTRACTOR. All costs incurred by the CONTRACTOR in preparing the schedule shall be borne by the CONTRACTOR as a part of its responsibility under this contract.

The initial schedule as approved by the GOVERNMENT and signed by the CONTRACTOR will become the official project schedule.

A. Preparation of Initial Schedule

Within 10 calendar days of the contract award, the CONTRACTOR shall meet with the GOVERNMENT'S expert to begin developing the initial schedule. Within 30 days of the contract award, the CONTRACTOR will complete development of the initial schedule and present to the OWNER an activity on arrow diagram depicting its schedule for computer processing by the GOVERNMENT.

Following computer processing and within 14 calendar days of submission of the diagram, the GOVERNMENT and CONTRACTOR shall meet for joint review, correction, and adjustment of the schedule. The construction time, as determined by the schedule, for the entire project or any milestone shall not exceed the specified contract time. In the event that any milestone date or contract completion date is exceeded in the schedule, logic and/or time estimates will be revised.

After any changes in the logic and/or time estimates have been agreed upon, another computerized schedule will be generated. The process will be repeated, if necessary, until the schedule meets all contractual requirements. However, the schedule must be finalized within 60 days of the Notice to Proceed. Failure to finalize the schedule by that date will result in withholding all contract payments until the schedule is finalized.

Scheduling Specification

Figure 4.4

Once the initial schedule has been finalized and is within contract requirements, the CONTRACTOR shall submit a signed copy of the schedule to the GOVERNMENT.

B. Schedule Requirements

All activity on arrow diagrams provided by the CONTRACTOR shall include:

    1. activity nodes

    2. activity description

    3. activity duration

The activity on arrow diagram shall show the sequence and interdependence of all activities required for complete performance of all items of work under this contract, including shop drawing submittals and approvals, and fabrication and delivery activities. All network "dummies" are to be shown on the diagram.

No activity duration shall be longer than 15 work days without the GOVERNMENT'S approval.

The GOVERNMENT reserves the right to limit the number of activities on the schedule.

The activities are to be described so that the work is readily identifiable and the progress on each activity can be readily measured. For each activity the CONTRACTOR shall identify the trade or subcontractor performing the work, the duration of the activity in work days, the manpower involved by trade, and the equipment and amount of material involved, and a dollar value of the activity. The dollar value assigned to each activity is to be reasonable and based on the amount of labor, materials, and equipment involved. When added together the dollar value of all activities are to equal the contract price.

The CONTRACTOR shall also provide the following information: work days per week, holidays, number of shifts per day, number of hours per shift, and major equipment to be used.

C. 60-Day Preliminary Schedule

Before proceeding with any work on site, the CONTRACTOR shall prepare, submit, and receive the GOVERNMENT'S approval of a 60-Day Preliminary Schedule. This schedule shall provide a detailed breakdown of activities scheduled for the first 60 days of the project and shall include mobilization, submittals, procurement, and construction.

Figure 4.4 (cont.)

No contract work may be pursued at the site without an approved 60-Day Preliminary Schedule or an approved CPM schedule.

D.   Schedule Updates and Progress Payments

Job site progress meeting will be held monthly by the GOVERNMENT and CONTRACTOR for the purpose of updating the project work schedule and determining the appropriate amount of partial payment due the CONTRACTOR. Progress will be reviewed to verify finish dates of completed activities, remaining duration of uncompleted activities, and any proposed logic and/or time estimate revisions. It is the CONTRACTOR'S responsibility to provide the GOVERNMENT with the status of activities at this progress meeting. The GOVERNMENT will process schedule updates based on this information once it has been verified.

The CONTRACTOR will submit revised activity on arrow diagrams for the following: delay in completion of any critical activity; actual prosecution of the work which is, as determined by the GOVERNMENT, significantly different than that represented on the schedule; or the addition, deletion, or revision of activities required by contract modification. The contract completion time will be adjusted only for causes specified in this contract.

As determined by CPM analysis, only delays in activities which affect milestone dates or contract completion dates will be considered for a time extension.

If the CONTRACTOR does seek a time extension of any milestone or contract completion date, it shall furnish documentation as required by the GOVERNMENT to enable the GOVERNMENT to determine whether a time extension is appropriate under the terms of the contract.

It is understood by the GOVERNMENT and CONTRACTOR that float is a shared commodity.

The principles involved and terms used in this section are as set forth in the Associated General Contractors of America publication, "The Use of CPM in Construction, A Manual for General Contractors and the Construction Industry," Copyright 1976.

There are numerous other types of submissions that the contract will require during the course of the project. The most frequent type of submission the contractor must prepare involves shop drawings.

Figure 4.4 (cont.)

Chapter Five
Changes

Chapter Five
Changes

A change is any difference between what was originally required by the contract documents and what may later be required of the contractor during construction. The prudent construction contractor should ensure that his entire staff understands the definition of a change and its importance in the context of a construction contract.

Changes to Construction Contracts

The construction contract differs from other types of contracts in the following way. Most other contracts represent a firm agreement between two parties. The construction contract, on the other hand, can be changed only *by the owner*, in this case, the government. The competitive bidding system is based on the assumption that the plans and specifications are reliable. Using these reliable specifications, one bidder will submit the lowest competitive bid. In reality, all parties to the contract recognize that plans and specifications are not perfect, and they expect changes to occur during the course of construction — after the contract has been signed.

There are many reasons why changes may occur. The first involves errors or omissions in the plans and specifications. As these errors and omissions are recognized, some corrective action may be required. If this corrective action deviates from the original contract requirements, it is considered a *change*. Second, the government agency may want to make alterations to the structure during the course of construction. Finally, government representatives may create a change situation by their actions or failure to act.

Changes caused by errors and omissions, alterations to the structure, or failure to act are all addressed by the *Changes Clause* in a government contract. It is important that a construction contractor who works for the government thoroughly understand the Changes Clause and all of its ramifications. While changes are generally addressed in the context of the Changes Clause, examples of other clauses in the federal contract under which a contractor may also receive compensation for changes are the *Differing Site Conditions*

Clause, explained later in this chapter, and the *Suspension of Work Clause*, described in Chapter 6.

In the next section of this chapter, the Changes Clause is described and an actual Changes Clause is shown. Then, various types and effects of changes that can occur in a construction project are listed and described. Both directed and constructive changes are covered. The following section in this chapter addresses the Differing Site Conditions Clause. Finally, the last part of the chapter contains information on how to provide the proper written notification for a change, and other general information concerning changes. Changes related to time are discussed in Chapter 6, and estimating the cost of changes is addressed in Chapter 7.

Changes Clause

In a construction contract, the government — by virtue of the Changes Clause — is given the right to make changes in the scope of the work during the course of construction. All construction contracts include a Changes Clause because no plans and specifications are perfect. The present federal Changes Clause is shown in Figure 5.1. As stated in paragraph (e) of the Changes Clause, the party performing the work agrees to perform that change work based on the understanding that equitable compensation will be received.

Directed Changes
The first and most common type of change allowed by the Changes Clause is a directed change, or a change that is clearly directed by the government. Some examples of directed changes are described in the following paragraphs.

Change in Quantity
The government may include a unit price item in the construction contract with a specified quantity for that item. If the quantity that is *actually* required either underruns or overruns the quantity *estimated* in the construction contract, this is construed as a change. As the Changes Clause notes, the equitable adjustment is based on the unit price specified in the contractor's initial bid.

The unit price originally specified in the contract may only change if the quantity is significantly altered. This situation is governed by the *Variations in Estimated Quantities Clause*, (shown in Figure 5.2), which states that when specified units vary in excess of 15% of the quantity stated in the contract, then either the government or the contractor is entitled to renegotiate the unit price. If the quantity of material units actually used in construction is significantly lower than that specified in the contract, the contractor's unit costs for that item will usually be higher and the unit price as bid can be renegotiated. Conversely, when there is a significant increase in quantity, the original bid unit price may overcompensate the contractor. Consequently, the government may renegotiate the unit price downward.

Changes Clause

a. The Contracting Officer may, at any time, without notice to the sureties, by written order designated or indicated to be a change order, make any changes in the work within the general scope of the contract, including but not limited to changes:

   i. in the specifications (including drawings and designs);

   ii. in the method or manner of performance of the work;

   iii. in the government-furnished facilities, equipment, materials, services, or site; or

   iv. directing acceleration in the performance of the work.

b. Any other written order or an oral order which terms as used in this paragraph b. shall include direction, instruction, interpretation or determination from the Contracting Officer, which causes any such change, shall be treated as a change order under this clause, provided that the Contractor gives the Contracting Officer written notice stating the date, circumstances, and source of the order that the contractor regards the order as a change order.

c. Except as herein provided, no order, statement, or conduct of the Contracting Officer shall be treated as a change under this clause or entitle the Contractor to an equitable adjustment hereunder.

d. If any change under this clause causes an increase or decrease in the Contractor's cost of, or the time required for, the performance of any part of the work under this contract, whether or not changed by any order, an equitable adjustment shall be made and the contract modified in writing accordingly: Provided, however, that except for claims based on defective specifications, no claim for any change under b. above shall be allowed for any costs incurred more than 20 days before the Contractor gives written notice as therein required: And provided further that in the case of defective specifications for which the government is responsible, the equitable adjustment shall include any increased cost reasonably incurred by the Contractor in attempting to comply with such defective specifications.

e. If the Contractor intends to assert a claim for an equitable adjustment under this clause, he must, within 30 days after receipt of a written change order under a. above or the furnishing of a written notice under b. above, submit to the Contracting Officer a written statement setting forth the general nature and monetary extent of such claim, unless this period is extended by the government. The statement of claim hereunder may be included in the notice under b. above.

f. No claim by the contractor for an equitable adjustment hereunder shall be allowed if asserted after final payment under this contract.

Figure 5.1

Items Not Included

Many other kinds of directed changes may occur in the course of construction. For example, the government may direct additional work in the form of *items not included* in the original contract documents, but which the government now recognizes are required or desired in the end product. Examples of this type of directed change are listed in Figure 5.3.

Generally, all of the above-listed changes are acknowledged as directed changes to the construction contract by the government, and the contractor may be entitled to additional compensation. If a dispute does arise, it usually involves the amount of the compensation that the contractor is seeking. The government representative may believe that the cost that the contractor requests is too high, that the change should be of no cost, or perhaps even that a credit is due to the government.

Directed changes to a construction contract are generally not major obstacles in the course of completing the project. However, directed changes do have the potential to cause delays, suspensions, inefficiencies, or changes in the contractor's sequence of activities. The construction contractor must accurately and thoroughly assess all the potential impacts of a change, including the cost for performing the work, and also the sequence or timing of the work. All possible impacts of the change must be assessed at the time that the change is presented in order to resolve the change completely.

Variations in Estimated Quantities Clause

Where the quantity of pay item in this contract is an estimated quantity and where the actual quantity of such pay item varies more than fifteen percent (15%) above or below the estimated quantity stated in this contract, an equitable adjustment in the contract price shall be made upon demand of either party. The equitable adjustment shall be based upon any increase or decrease in costs due solely to the variation above one hundred fifteen percent (115%) or below eighty-five percent (85%) of the estimated quantity. If the quantity variation is such as to cause an increase in the time necessary for completion, the Contracting Officer shall, upon receipt of a written request for an extension of time within ten (10) days from the beginning of such delays, or within such further period of time which may be granted by the Contracting Officer prior to the date of final settlement of the contract, ascertain the facts and make such adjustment for extending the completion date as in his judgment the findings justify.

Figure 5.2

Constructive Changes

The most difficult type of change in a construction project is a *constructive change*. Constructive changes are those which the government constructively, or effectively, creates by its actions or lack of action. For example, if the government fails to perform a task specified by the contract, a change will result.

There are many other types of constructive changes. Some of the more common types are listed and described in the following pages. The selection that follows is by no means exhaustive, but rather is intended to give the reader an idea of the areas or the types of constructive changes that may occur on a construction project.

Late Inspection

One type of constructive change is known as late inspection. Late inspection occurs when the government fails to perform a required inspection within the time limits mandated by the contract. For example, a construction contractor working for the government is required by the contract to install an underground pipeline or utility. The contract also requires that the pipeline be inspected by a government inspector *before* the contractor

Examples of Directed Changes

- The government may add additional lighting fixtures throughout the facility.
- The government may upgrade the capacities of electrical or mechanical equipment in the facility.
- The government may add fire protection systems, alarm systems, or telephone systems throughout the facility which were not originally specified in the contract.
- The government may direct the contractor to complete the project ahead of schedule or in a time frame ending earlier than the required contract completion date. These cases are referred to as *directed acceleration*.
- The government may alter or direct a contractor to change the method of performing the work. For instance, the contractor may have originally planned to excavate by blasting rock at the project site. At some point before, or even after work has begun, the government may direct that the rock be removed by mechanical means rather than blasting for various reasons not specified in the contract documents.
- The government may upgrade the size and capacity of structural members throughout the facility.
- The government may upgrade the quality of some of the finishes throughout the facility, such as floor coverings, wall coverings, ceiling treatment, or trim.

Figure 5.3

backfills the trench, and that the government inspector shall be available to inspect the pipeline within a 24-hour notice period. If the contractor notifies the government representative at ten o'clock on a Tuesday morning that a certain segment of the pipeline is ready to be inspected, the government inspector must inspect that pipeline by ten o'clock on Wednesday morning. If the government inspector does not show up on Tuesday or by ten o'clock on Wednesday morning, this is considered a change because it differs from what the contract required.

In this example, the government caused the change and is responsible for it because the contractor properly requested the inspection, but the government did not fulfill its obligation and inspect in a timely fashion. The government's *lack of action* caused the change. Therefore, the government effectively, or constructively, changed the contract, thus the term *constructive changes*.

Late inspection can have many repercussions. For instance, the contractor may have had a crew standing by waiting for the inspector to show up so that they could proceed with the backfilling. The contractor may also have mobilized equipment in anticipation of resuming work after the inspection. In this case, the equipment would have been idle and would represent additional cost. In the worst case, rain may have washed mud into the trench and contaminated the bedding, thereby forcing the contractor to remove the pipe, then remove the bedding, and replace it with new bedding material. In such cases, the contractor must define all the impacts of the late inspection and define these impacts in terms of cost.

Higher Standard of Performance
A higher standard of performance change generally relates to a defective specification or, in other words, a specification that does not completely detail what is required on the project. In this situation, the government, in an effort to obtain what is needed, requires the contractor to provide or perform to a higher standard than originally specified in the contract.

An example of a higher standard of performance change can be seen in a project constructed for the Corps of Engineers. The project was primarily horizontal construction, earthwork. The specifications required the contractor, when backfilling, to compact the material by making three passes with a sheep's foot roller or similar specified compaction equipment. When the contractor had completed the backfilling operation, the Corps of Engineers representative took Proctor tests of the compacted material. At that time, the Corps decided that the material had to meet a 90% modified Proctor test and directed the contractor to perform whatever work was necessary so that the material, when compacted, would pass this test. The contract had required only that the contractor make three passes with a sheep's foot roller. The constructive requirement, to pass a 90% modified Proctor test, was not specified in the contract documents. Hence this is a constructive change because it requires the contractor to meet a higher standard than what was originally specified.

Improper Rejection

Closely associated with a higher standard of performance is another constructive change known as improper rejection. With this type of constructive change, the government representative improperly concludes that the material, methods, or workmanship of the contractor do not meet the standards of the specifications and, consequently, require the contractor to do more work or some other type of work. In the example given for a higher standard of performance, the contractor was eventually required to meet a Proctor test for compaction. The original specifications for backfilling (three passes of a sheep's foot roller) were rejected. This is a case of improper rejection since the work performed met the requirements in the contract specifications.

At times, improper rejection occurs when the government or its designer desires a specific type of equipment or type of material. Because the government is limited in its ability to draft a sole source specification, it will instead draft a specification naming one material or one product, and stating that it will accept an approved equal. However, when the contractor attempts to perform the work, *no* other material or product is approved as equal. If other products or materials are, in fact, equal based on the criteria established and the wording of the clause, then it is an improper rejection.

Impossibility of Performance

Impossibility of performance is another type of constructive change. In this situation, the work cannot be performed as it is specified. It may not necessarily be technically impossible, but it may be practically impossible, or commercially impractical. The government may require work or effort that is either extremely expensive or unusually difficult to perform — beyond that which could be anticipated by a bidder based on the contract documents.

An example of impossibility of performance is a dispute which came before the General Services Board of Contract Appeals (GSBCA). In this case, with Kaplan Contractors, Inc. [GSBCA No. 2747, October 12, 1970], the General Services Administration specified the use of fiberglass prefabricated panels for the construction of lookout galleries in a post office. The contract named a specific supplier of these panels, or approved equal. The contractor was unable to locate any other supplier of the panels and based its bid on a quote from the named supplier. Once the contract work began, problems immediately arose concerning the panels. The supplier was late in supplying them and, of the panels delivered, approximately forty percent were rejected. Shortly thereafter, the supplier went out of business. The contractor located an alternate supplier whose panels did not meet the specification requirements. The GSA accepted the substitution as a "minor modification" to the contract, or one which would not require a change in the specifications. The contractor completed the work under protest at a much higher cost and submitted a claim for the increased cost.

In its decision, the GSBCA found that the government specified a proprietary item, available only from one supplier. The supplier's failure to perform made the contract impossible to carry out as written. Further, the government's acceptance of the substitution was an implied, or constructive, change and the contractor was entitled to additional compensation.

Withholding Material Information

Another example of a constructive change is known as failure to disclose material information, or withholding material information. The government has an obligation to inform the contractor of information which may affect the contractor's method or manner of performance of the work. If the government withholds such information, it may lead to a constructive change to the contract.

For example, a contract required the construction of a tunnel and the installation of a conveyor system in the tunnel to remove tailings from a mining operation. The contractor who was awarded the job planned to use a tunnel boring machine to construct the tunnel. When the operation began, excessive voids were encountered, at which time it was disclosed that there was an abandoned mine shaft intersecting the path of the new tunnel. The contractor was forced to remove the tunnel boring machine from the project and to "drill and shoot" the tunnel from both ends. This revised approach resulted in tremendous extra cost and delay to the contractor. The government had full knowledge of the existence of the abandoned mine shaft, but failed to provide this information to any of the bidders on the project. This is a change resulting from the withholding of material information.

In a similar case, the federal government contracted to have an addition built for an office building in Washington, D.C. When the contractor began excavation on the foundations, he encountered a large concrete loading dock. It became known later that the government had full knowledge of this loading dock, but for alleged security reasons had not revealed this information to the bidders. The contractor sought recovery based on a *differing site condition change*. However, this situation also represents a constructive change in that the owner failed to disclose this piece of material information.

A Final Word on Constructive Changes

The reason constructive changes most often end up in dispute is simple. For the government to agree that a constructive change has occurred, it also must admit that it made a mistake. In the example where the government required a 90% modified Proctor compaction but did not specify this requirement, it had to admit that its plans and specifications were defective, or that it made a mistake. To avoid the difficulties of admitting that mistake, the government may state that "a knowledgeable contractor should have known that this was what was required," or "this is normal in the construction industry and you should have anticipated it," or any number of other responses. As a result, constructive changes often become disputes. Another problem is that many construction contractors do not recognize constructive changes when they occur and/or fail to give notice to the government that they are occurring. Providing proper written notice is discussed in more detail later in this chapter.

The aforementioned examples of constructive changes by no means represent the entire list of constructive changes that may occur. Other constructive changes related to time are described in Chapter 6. The construction contractor must be keenly aware that he is required to perform that which is specified in the contract documents. A deviation from those requirements is a change, whether it be a *directed change* or a *constructive change.*

Differing Site Conditions Clause

The Differing Site Conditions Clause, while distinct from the Changes Clause, provides another vehicle by which a contractor may receive additional compensation for extra work on a project. This clause is written as shown in Figure 5.4.

In federal construction contracts, two types of differing site conditions are generally recognized. Each is explained in the following paragraphs as Type I and Type II Differing Site Conditions.

Differing Site Conditions

a. The Contractor shall promptly, and before such conditions are disturbed, notify the Contracting Officer in writing of: (1) subsurface or latent physical conditions at the site, of an unusual nature, differing materially from those indicated in this contract, or (2) unknown physical conditions at the site, of an unusual nature, differing materially from those ordinarily encountered and generally recognized as inhering in work of the character provided for in this contract. The Contracting Officer shall promptly investigate the conditions, and if he finds that such conditions do materially so differ and cause an increase or decrease in the Contractor's cost of, or the time required for, performance of any part of the work under this contract, whether or not changed as a result of such conditions, an equitable adjustment shall be made and the contract modified in writing accordingly.

b. No claim of the Contractor under this clause shall be allowed unless the Contractor has given the notice required in a. above; provided, however, the time prescribed therefore may be extended by the government.

c. No claim by the Contractor for an equitable adjustment hereunder shall be allowed if asserted after final payment under this contract.

Figure 5.4

Type I

A Type I differing site condition is a condition that differs *materially* from that represented in the contract documents. In this case, the contractor encounters conditions at the site different from those represented by the contract documents. For example, soil information contained in a contract may not specify rock at a site. However, when the contractor begins excavating the site, he may encounter a significant amount of rock. This situation would be considered a Type I differing site condition. Likewise, if the contract documents state that an existing concrete slab has a specified thickness of eight inches, but the contractor begins demolition of the slab and discovers that it is in excess of 18 inches, this is another Type I differing site condition.

The following example is of a Type I differing site condition resolved before the Agriculture Board of Contract Appeals (AGBCA). [AGBCA 76-109] The contractor was required by the contract to backfill trenches and compact the material to 95% density. The contract further specified that the "contractor may obtain" the material from a borrow pit shown on the plans. When the contractor attempted to utilize the material from the pit, it was not of the proper gradation and could not be reasonably compacted to 95% density. Consequently, the contractor requested additional compensation under the Differing Site Conditions Clause.

The government agency denied compensation, stating that the quality of the material was not guaranteed and that the agency was not obligated to provide material. The Agricultural Board of Appeals (AGBCA), however, ruled in favor of the contractor, noting that although the government was not required to provide material, since it did, there was an implied warranty that the material would be adequate. Therefore, the contractor had a right to rely on the accuracy of the contract documents and should be compensated because of the differing site condition.

Type II

A Type II differing site condition is a condition of an unusual nature not ordinarily anticipated for that type of work in that area of the country. For example, a contractor may have excavated to install a pipeline. The material encountered may have been that specified in the contract documents, but the soil below the pipe may behave in a way different from that which anyone could have anticipated. If the soil is not capable of supporting the pipe, the pipe, as installed, would sink. The behavior of the soil could not have been anticipated by the contractor or the government. Thus, it fits into the Type II differing site condition category.

Documenting a Change

The changes clauses require that a contractor who encounters a change on a project notify the government of that change in a timely manner. The reason for timely notification is to allow the owner (the government) the opportunity to assess the following conditions:

1. Whether or not the situation is, in fact, a change
2. The best course of action it can take to resolve that change
3. Ways in which the costs of the change can be mitigated

The government's aim is to resolve the problem at the least cost. A contractor who fails to give proper notice of the change may lose the right to recover the extra cost associated with that change. All contractors doing work with the government should train and educate their staff — at all levels — as to what constitutes a change, and the methods for providing the government with proper and timely notification.

Written Notice

In giving notice to the government, it should not be presumed that "anything will suffice." In a case decided by the Department of the Interior Board of Contract Appeals (IBCA), a contractor argued that his company's invoice served as adequate notice to the government of an anticipated cost overrun on a cost-plus contract which had a Limitation of Cost Clause. The IBCA ruled that the invoice was not adequate notice and the contractor was not entitled to additional compensation.

The letter giving notice of a change should be very clear and precise, and should document the occurrences that resulted in the change. The contractor must show that what is now being required is different from that which the contract originally required. A notice letter must specify all the facts surrounding the change, the dates when the actions were first initiated by the government, the circumstances giving rise to the change and, perhaps most importantly, the impact of that change. Some of the effects of extra work might include a reduction in the efficiency of the contractor's labor or equipment or a delay to the project that causes additional costs. Finally, after specifying the impacts, the contractor should identify, as well as possible, the specific costs associated with the change. The contractor should also include a statement reserving the right to request compensation for costs that cannot be anticipated at that time or for impacts that cannot be foreseen. The following is an example of such a statement.

> "The impacts and costs noted above include only those items which can presently be determined. We reserve our rights to request compensation for any future impacts and costs which might arise or be caused by this change."

Figure 5.5 is a sample notice letter. The notice letter includes specific facts, circumstances, dates, impacts, and costs. Figure 5.6 is the same standard notice letter, but with the specific facts, dates, impacts, and costs deleted. This form is a sample letter to be used by a field project manager or office project manager, who need only "fill in the blanks." It is strongly suggested that all contracting organizations consider including a standard notice

```
United States Army
Corps of Engineers
New Orleans District
New Orleans, LA  xxxxx

ATT:  Colonel John Doe
      Contracting Officer

RE:   Contract DACW xxxx, Dam Modification

Dear Colonel Doe:

With respect to the project captioned above, we wish to advise you
that a potential change condition exists. We trust that this prompt
notice will give the Government ample opportunity to resolve the
problem and provide us with the appropriate course of action. While
we do not intend to attempt to present all the facts surrounding the
problem, let us summarize the salient points.

On Thursday, January 27, we began installing the gate valves on the
project. The project has eight gate valves which rest on stainless
steel tracks which are cast into the structure. (Refer to Drawing No.
XYZ for details and Specification section PQR.) When we set the first
gate valve, we noted that the valve could not be opened to its full
position due to interference from the steel cross bracing above it.
We have verified that the cross bracing was constructed in accordance
with the contract requirements (refer to Drawing No. UST and
Specification section RST). We advised the Resident Engineer of the
situation and were directed by him to cease installation procedures
until the problem can be resolved.

We recognize that there are numerous approaches to the resolution of
this problem. Therefore, we cannot proceed until the Government gives
us clear direction. In the meantime, we have placed the other seven
gate valves in storage in a trailer on site.

The time for the crew and equipment to shut down and place the valves
in storage is shown in the attached sheets, along with the
corresponding costs. These costs total $872.15. Although this
activity is not on the project's critical path, we require a prompt
response since it has only twenty-two days of float and could rapidly
become critical. Once we are given clear direction as to how this
situation will be resolved, we will submit a cost estimate for same.
In the meantime, we request reimbursement for the costs noted above.
We will submit a formal change order proposal form in the next two
days.

We trust this provides you adequate information and notice for this
problem. Please let me know if you desire additional information.

                              Sincerely,


                              Project Manager

JJ/lc
Enclosure
cc: Resident Engineer
```

Sample Notice Letter

Figure 5.5

```
United States Army
Corps of Engineers
        District
        xxxxxxxx

ATT:  Colonel
      Contracting Officer

RE:   Contract DACW xxxx,

Dear Colonel _____:

With respect to the project captioned above, we wish to advise you
that a potential change condition exists. We trust that this prompt
notice will give the Government ample opportunity to resolve the
problem and provide us with the appropriate cause of action.

While we do not intend to attempt to present all of the facts
surrounding the problem, let me summarize the salient points.

We advised the Resident Engineer of the situation and were directed
by him to


Once we are given clear direction as to how this situation will be
resolved, we will submit a cost estimate. We will submit a formal
change order proposal form in the next two days.

We trust this provides you adequate information and notice for this
problem. Please let me know if you desire additional information.

                            Sincerely,



                            Joe Jack
                            Project Manager


JJ/lc

cc:  Resident Engineer
```

Sample Notice Letter

Figure 5.6

letter in their company procedures manual. In this way, the staff will understand and have an example of how to issue proper notice.

Estimating Impacts

Every change order that is executed with the government includes two elements, a cost and a time element. Questions of cost and time should not be left until the end of the job. These elements should be presented to the government in a formal letter of notice. Construction contractors often write letters explaining the change, but not specifying the impacts or the costs. Their reasoning is that they are not able to define the costs until they perform the work. If a contractor truly cannot estimate a cost or define the impacts because the change is not fully defined, he should notify the government — by letter — that a change condition exists and should state that the cost and impacts will be defined when the resolution of the change has been clearly defined by the government.

Estimating Cost

The majority of changes that occur are defined clearly enough for a contractor to assess the impacts and estimate the costs. It is always in the best interest of the contractor and the government to define the cost of the change as soon as possible. Using the estimated cost approach significantly reduces the incidence of disputes. Estimating the cost of changes is described in more detail in Chapter 7, "Pricing Changes."

Time Limits

In most changes clauses, there is a stated time limit within which notice must be given. A Changes Clause under the Federal Acquisition Regulation requires that notice be given within 30 days of the contractor's becoming aware of the change condition.

The main reason for a time limit is to ensure that the government's actions are not prejudiced in the resolution of a change. The concept of timeliness and prejudice is simple. If a contractor fails to give notice within the required time frame, the question is, does that untimeliness limit the government's options in deciding how to handle the change? If there were ways in which the government could have prevented or reduced costs that have already been incurred, then indeed the government's rights have been prejudiced. If, on the other hand, the contractor gives notice after the 30-day time limit, yet this lateness does not reduce the government's options, then there is no prejudice of the government's rights.

If the government refuses to grant additional compensation because the contractor did not give timely notice, the contractor must be able to demonstrate that the failure to give notice within the specified time limits did not prejudice the government's rights. Armed with proper evidence, the contractor can generally still recover compensation. Again, the prudent contractor will avoid these complications by giving notice within the time frame specified.

A contractor who has given notice of a change should not wait for the government to take action. Government representatives may have other pressing matters to manage and may not respond promptly to the contractor's letter of notice. For this reason, the contractor should establish a filing system and regular procedures for following up a letter of notice to the government. The contractor's objective is to resolve this potential change as quickly as possible by generating a formal change order from the government.

Actual or Imputed Knowledge

Although change notices are required in writing, a contractor who fails to give notice in writing is not entirely precluded from recovering the extra cost associated with the change. If the contractor is able to show that the government had actual or imputed knowledge of the change, then the contractor may be able to recover the additional costs.

What constitutes actual or imputed knowledge? The minutes of a job progress meeting represent a good example since they indicate that a contractor effectively gave verbal notice of a change. This evidence clearly proves that the owner had knowledge of the change. Alternately, if it can be shown that the owner directed a change by letter or some other correspondence, then, once again, it is evident that the owner had knowledge that a change was in progress. However, it is always in the contractor's best interest to give formal written notice of a change regardless of any discussion that has occurred.

Change Order Proposal Log

All too often, construction projects involve numerous change order proposals. The administrative and bookkeeping tasks are increased as a result. For this reason, many contractors find it worthwhile to maintain a *change order proposal log*. Each change order proposal, when submitted to the government, is assigned a specific number so that the contractor can readily identify it as time goes on. As a change order proposal is resolved as a change order, it should be cross-referenced. A log should be kept of change orders that are pending and those that are resolved. The contractor and staff must stay on top of the status of all change order proposals and change orders to insure that nothing "falls between the cracks." While maintaining change order records can be a cumbersome task, it is one that is absolutely necessary to the efficient management of changes on a government contract.

Defective Design

Contractors should be careful how they present a change which they feel was due to problems in the plans and specifications. It may not be in the contractor's best interest to label the cause of a problem as a *defective design*. In presenting any potential change, the contractor should avoid, at all costs, pointing a finger at any specific party or placing blame on anyone. Such a claim may alienate the project designer who is likely to be actively involved in the resolution of changes as they occur. The contractor should view all changes in the same manner: the contract required A; the Government has now required B, which is different from A; therefore, this is a change. The request for a change and all correspondence for that change should be expressed in neutral terms. Problems should be addressed simply as a change — something different from what the contract required. Trying to point out the cause of the problem does not help the contractor resolve the problem.

Continuation of Work

All too often, changes are not resolved before the work is performed. Government representatives may not have time to process the paperwork and may direct that the work be performed and the paperwork resolved later. Or, contractors may delay submitting accurate cost breakdowns to the government when they are given a request for a cost and pricing proposal for potential change work. Contractors should, however, respond to government cost proposals as quickly as possible in order to increase the chances that the change will be resolved before the work is performed.

A contractor may be directed by the government to proceed with a change even if a formal change order with an agreed price has not been developed. A literal reading of the Changes Clause leads one to conclude that before a contractor performs any extra work, he must first have an executed change order with the government. However, the Changes Clause clearly states that if the government and the contractor are not able to reach an agreement on the change order, then the government may direct the contractor to perform the work. Generally referred to as "continuation of work," this phrasing is included in all government contracts so that projects will not be unnecessarily delayed due to disagreements regarding a change. While the contractor, if directed, must continue the work, he should also maintain accurate cost records and detailed documentation of all of the work associated with that change.

If the change is not resolved even after the work has been performed, the contractor should consider certifying the change as a *claim* in accordance with the Contract Disputes Act of 1978. (Management of disputes is discussed in greater detail in Chapters 10 and 11.)

Alternative Procedures

There are times in government contracting when the government and the contractor may agree that a change exists, but cannot agree on the impacts of the change or the cost associated with those impacts. In those cases, a variety of procedures may be followed, some of which are described in the following sections.

Two-Part Modification

When the government and the contractor cannot agree on the cost of a change, the government may issue a two-part modification. The first part is issued under a specific modification number and labeled *Part One*. Part One explains the change and the cost to which the government and the contractor have agreed. The contractor may then requisition against that amount of money and be paid up to that amount once the work has been performed.

When the government and the contractor resolve the remaining questions on the change, that agreement becomes *Part Two*, the second and final part of the modification. Changes that have impacts, such as delays or inefficiencies, fall into this category.

The government resolves the direct cost as Part One of the modification. Once an analysis has been performed on the inefficiencies, delays, and delay damages, then that resolution becomes Part Two of the modification.

Unilateral Change Order

In most cases, a change order is executed by both the government and the contractor and is a *bilateral* agreement. However, if the government and the contractor cannot agree on the cost of the change order, then the government may issue a *unilateral* change order, signed only by the government. The unilateral change order states what the government agrees to as the cost of the change. The contractor can requisition against this dollar amount when the work is performed. However, the contractor still retains his rights for compensation for additional costs or impacts to which he feels entitled, but to which the government has not yet agreed.

Reservation of Rights Clause

The Reservation of Rights Clause reserves the contractor's rights to request or claim additional costs or damages associated with the other impacts of a change, such as delays or inefficiencies. Some government agencies accept the changes clause with a reservation of rights, others do not. The policy varies from agency to agency and also within the administering office of each agency. If a contractor insists on including a Reservation of Rights Clause and the government is unwilling to accept it, then the contractor should discuss with the government a two-part modification or a unilateral modification. By including one of these modifications, the contractor can at least be paid for the costs to which the government agrees for the change work.

Change Order Limits and Audits

If a contractor has a change order in excess of certain limits, an audit may be required by the government agency. For agencies other than the Department of Defense, the threshold is $100,000. The limit for Department of Defense agencies has recently been upgraded to $500,000. If a change order proposal exceeds the specified limit, the contractor must be audited prior to the resolution of that change. Normally, the contractor will be required to certify that his cost and pricing data are accurate and not fraudulent. The audit is usually performed by an agency outside that with which the construction contract exists. This is because the agencies' resources are "generally" limited in terms of their ability to conduct audits. (See Chapter 8 for a more detailed discussion of audits.)

The Role of Other Professionals

Most of this chapter addresses changes generically from the general contractor's perspective. However, it should be noted that subcontractors, design professionals, and government representatives are also affected by changes.

Subcontractors

A subcontractor or supplier on a construction project with the government does not have any contractual agreement with the government, but is instead bound by the terms of his agreement with the general contractor. If the subcontractor/supplier experiences changes as previously described, he should notify the general contractor who can, in turn, give notice to the government.

While a subcontractor/supplier does not have the legal right to pursue remedies directly against the government, requests/claims are usually "passed through" to government representatives by the general contractor. Thus, the subcontractor/supplier should also be knowledgeable concerning both directed and constructive changes and the mandated contract procedures to resolve them.

Generally, subcontract agreements incorporate by reference the conditions of the general contract. A subcontractor/supplier's failure to give notice may, therefore, negate his eligibility to be compensated for changes.

Design Services

The design professional working for the federal government has a two-fold perspective on changes. First, the designer is sometimes required to perform work beyond the contract requirements. This would constitute a change to the designer's contract. Second, the designer may cause or initiate some of the constructive changes previously discussed.

In the first circumstance, the designer must have a clear understanding of the requirements of his contract with the government. These requirements relate to the "Statement of Work" or "Scope of Work" defined in the contract. All too often, these statements are not defined as specifically as they should be. The designer must insure that the scope of work is described as clearly as possible, particularly with respect to responsibilities concerning review of shop drawings, submittals, and duties during the construction phase of the project.

The federal contract for design services usually states that the designer must provide a design that will be bid within the government budget. If the competitive bids exceed the budget, the government may require the designer to modify or redesign the project in order to meet the budgetary constraints. Such redesign work is at no cost to the government. If, however, the government requires additional design work to modify the project due to government-initiated changes, the designer is entitled to additional compensation, resolved in accordance with the Changes Clause in the design contract.

With respect to constructive changes, it is better for the design professional to admit a possible error than to adamantly maintain a position that will lead to a more expensive change. The government has adopted an aggressive policy of seeking compensation from the design professional for changes due to design negligence. A literal interpretation of present policy requires all agencies to review each construction change order for potential design liability. Given that exposure, the designer is well advised to pay particular attention to its role as the cause of constructive changes.

The Government Representative

The federal employee, the government's representative, has control over many of the situations that give rise to changes, both directed and constructive. He has the ability to reduce both the incidence of changes and their cost. The government representative should understand what constitutes a change and be familiar with the multitude of constructive changes that can occur.

The government representative has the ability to reduce the incidence of changes by observing the following practices: reviewing the design prior to bid, conducting meaningful pre-bid and pre-construction meetings, and responding to requests for information, submittals, and shop drawings in a timely fashion. In addition, the final cost of a change can be reduced if the government acts promptly to resolve the situation once a change is recognized.

To properly and effectively manage changes, the government representative must maintain an objective viewpoint and understand and accept that no set of plans and specifications is perfect and, consequently, changes will occur. Some government representatives tend to think that every request for a change signals an attempt by the contractor or designer to get additional compensation without justification. However, by being open-minded and reasonable, the government representative can significantly reduce the incidence of disputes and can reward the government with a more cost-effective project overall.

Summary

All contractors for government projects should ensure that their entire staffs are thoroughly educated in the administration and/or management of changes on a government contract. They should know what constitutes a change, both directed and constructive. The staff must understand that if there is a potential change, they should immediately notify the government agency, and follow up by submitting the proper documentation to the government as soon as possible.

The change order procedures represent a complicated, but crucial process. The steps that must be taken are summarized in a flow chart shown in Figure 5.7.

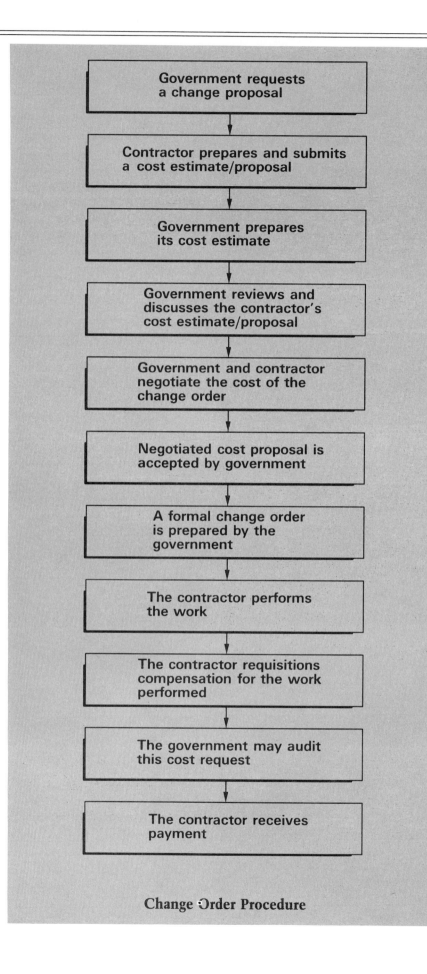

Change Order Procedure

Figure 5.7

Chapter Six
Time-Related Changes

Chapter Six
Time-Related Changes

In the recent past, problems with time extensions and delays to government construction projects have become tremendous. In fact, the largest dollar value disputes are the result of delay damage claims. To avoid such disputes, all parties to a construction contract should have a clear understanding of time in construction and all of its related implications. In this chapter, we will address the issue of time-related changes. We will discuss types of delays, how to perform a delay analysis, and time-related disputes. We will also address changes in the sequence of work and accelerations. We will begin with the Suspension of Work Clause, the government's formal mechanism for allowing a delay in a project.

Suspension of Work Clause

Suspension of work is a type of change that affects not only the completion date of a project, but also its cost. The government contract allows for changes specifically related to time through the Suspension of Work Clause, shown in Figure 6.1.

It is not a common occurrence for the government to suspend a construction project. It is far more common for the government to effect a *constructive suspension of work*. A constructive suspension of work is a delay resulting from a *constructive change*, that is, a change brought about by the government's action, or lack of action.

Some of the constructive changes mentioned in Chapter 5 may well cause delays or an effective suspension of work to a project. However, there are also other actions or lack of action on the part of the government which may lead to constructive suspensions. For example, government contracts often specify a maximum duration for the review and approval of shop drawings by the government or its design consultant. If the government exceeds that time frame, it may cause a constructive suspension to the project or to a portion of the work on the project. This situation also applies to government-required actions on product information, material submissions, and samples. Inspection requirements, discussed in Chapter 5, may also cause a constructive suspension.

Changing the Sequence of Work

Besides delays or suspensions of work, the government may also effect a constructive change by altering the *sequence* of the contractor's work. The sequence of work may be altered in many ways. For example, the constructive changes described in Chapter 5 might well affect the contractor's sequence of work. Likewise, the government's failure to provide information requested by the contractor on the drawings, or to release a portion of the drawings, may alter the contractor's sequence of work. Similarly, the sequence could be altered if the government fails to approve some of the contractor's submissions or work plans, or does not approve them in a timely fashion. If the government does not provide full access to the site, this too may affect the contractor's sequence of work.

Suspension of Work Clause

a. The Contracting Officer may order the Contractor in writing to suspend, delay, or interrupt all or any part of the work for such period of time as he may determine to be appropriate for the convenience of the government.

b. If the performance of all or any part of the work is, for an unreasonable period of time, suspended, delayed, or interrupted by an act of the Contracting Officer in the administration of this contract, or by his failure to act within the time specified in this contract (or if no time is specified, within a reasonable time), an adjustment shall be made for any increase in the cost of performance of this contract (excluding profit) necessarily caused by such unreasonable suspension, delay, or interruption and the contract modified in writing accordingly. However, no adjustment shall be made under this clause for any suspension, delay, or interruption to the extent (1) that performance would have been so suspended, delayed, or interrupted by any other cause, including the fault or negligence of the Contractor or (2) for which an equitable adjustment is provided for or excluded under any other provision of this contract.

c. No claim under this clause shall be allowed (1) for any costs incurred more than 20 days before the Contractor shall have notified the Contracting Officer in writing of the act or failure to act involved (but this requirement shall not apply as to a claim resulting from a suspension order), and (2) unless the claim, in an amount stated, is asserted in writing as soon as practicable after the termination of such suspension, delay, or interruption, but not later than the date of final payment under the contract.

Figure 6.1

Constructive Acceleration

Another time-related change is constructive acceleration, the result of a constructive change. The six basic conditions for constructive acceleration are listed below.

1. The contractor has experienced an excusable delay.
2. The contractor has given notice of this excusable delay to the government and has requested a time extension.
3. The government has refused to grant a time extension.
4. The contractor is directed by the government to finish on time.
5. The contractor accelerates the project in one form or another in order to meet the project deadline.
6. The contractor incurs additional costs due to the acceleration.

Types of Delays

Two types of delays occur on construction projects — *excusable delays* and *non-excusable delays*. To determine which category a delay falls into, one must identify the party liable for the delay. This information is the basis for deciding whether or not a contractor is entitled to a time extension, and if the contractor is to be compensated for the delay.

Non-Excusable Delays
Non-excusable delays are those that are foreseeable, or are within the control of the contractor. When a non-excusable delay occurs, the contractor is not entitled to a time extension. Furthermore, if the project finishes late because of the non-excusable delay, the contractor is liable for liquidated damages to the federal government. Examples of non-excusable delays are listed below.

- A subcontractor does not perform on time.
- A supplier does not provide material in a timely fashion.
- The general contractor does not expedite the work promptly.

Excusable Delays
Excusable delays are unforeseeable delays which are beyond the control of the contractor. Excusable delays are divided into two categories — *non-compensable* and *compensable*.

Non-Compensable Delays
Neither the contractor nor the government has control over a non-compensable delay, such as unusually severe weather or a strike. The contractor is entitled to a time extension, but is not given any monetary compensation. The contractor absorbs any costs associated with being on the project longer, while the government absorbs its cost by claiming liquidated damages because of the time extension.

Typical non-compensable delays are strikes, and acts of God, such as unusually severe weather, fires, floods, and other disasters. It should be noted that non-compensable delays granted for weather problems apply only to *unusually* severe weather; in other words, only weather that is not anticipated at that time of year in that part of the country. The contractor is not entitled to a time extension for inclement weather if those conditions are typical for the region and time of year. The criteria for unusually severe weather is based upon a review of the historical weather data for that area. Historical weather data may be obtained from the National Oceanic and Atmospheric Administration (NOAA) or a similar agency. This weather data is usually compiled from the preceding five-year period.

Sometimes, even proof of unusually severe weather does not warrant a time extension. The contractor must demonstrate that the unusually severe weather actually delayed the critical path work of the project (discussed later in this chapter). For example, if the building is already enclosed and the unusually severe weather could have no effect on the contractor's work, then a time extension would not be warranted.

Unusually severe weather can cause a delay that is greater than the duration of the severe weather itself. For example, if a contractor is performing site work and experiences two days of unusually severe rain, the site may become so saturated that work cannot be resumed for five or six days. Consequently, the time extension requested is for the five or six days, the amount of time that the contractor was actually delayed because of the unusually severe weather.

Some federal agencies, particularly the Corps of Engineers, specify in their construction contracts what the "normal" weather is for that area, particularly with regard to precipitation. In fact, many Corps of Engineers' contracts state how many days of a specified amount of rain are expected for each month of the year in that part of the country. If the amount of rain exceeds the number specified in the contract, then it is considered unusually severe weather. The contract must be read carefully in order to determine these allowances.

Non-compensable delays may also occur at the subcontractor or supplier level. Such delays may affect the general contractor and, therefore, represent valid non-compensable delays. For instance, if a major supplier experiences tornado damage to its plant, preventing it from operating for three days, and the three days of delay affect a critical activity on the general contractor's schedule, this delay warrants a time extension. Similarly, labor strikes among subcontractors that affect a critical activity on the general contractor's schedule would warrant a request for a time extension.

Compensable Delays
Compensable delays are unforeseeable delays beyond the contractor's control for which the contractor is entitled to a time extension and additional compensation. Generally, a compensable delay is caused by the government itself, through vehicles such as a direct change order, suspension of work, or any other constructive change. In order to receive compensation for the time extension, a contractor must demonstrate that the government was the cause of that delay.

Contractors generally base their bids on the anticipated start date of a contract. A delay in the start of the contract may increase the contractor's costs. These costs are recoverable if the contractor was not informed of the delay. However, these costs are *not* recoverable if the contractor is aware of the new date and has signed a contract with the later date on it. [Eng BCA No. 5203, January 16, 1987]

It is often difficult to define a delay in order to assign it to one of the three categories — non-excusable, excusable non-compensable, and excusable compensable. One such situation is shown in the following example. A construction contractor is erecting a building with a steel structural system for the federal government. The contractor chooses a steel supplier who agrees to fabricate and deliver the steel within three months but, in fact, delivers the steel in six months. Although this may appear to be an excusable delay if it delays activities on the critical path, the government may consider it a non-excusable delay because the contractor chose the supplier. The government's position might be that the contractor should have expedited the supplier or chosen a different supplier in order to meet the required schedule. If the specifications had required that the contractor purchase the steel from an identified supplier, and then that supplier was late in delivering the steel, however, it could be argued that the delay should be compensable. In this case, the contractor would have to demonstrate that it issued a requisition or purchase order in a timely fashion to the designated supplier and would have to prove that the supplier had indicated that it could provide the material within the scheduled time period. In yet another version, if the contractor chose the steel supplier, and the steel supplier was delayed because of a strike at its plant, this would be an excusable, but non-compensable, delay because neither the contractor, the supplier, nor the government had control over the strike.

Concurrent Delays

It is not uncommon on a construction project for more than one delay to occur at the same time. These are known as *concurrent delays*. For example, a contractor working on a federal government construction project experiences a strike by its trades that lasts for 30 days. At the same time, the government orders a suspension of work on the project starting on the first day of the strike and ending on the last day of the strike. The strike represents an excusable, non-compensable delay and the suspension of work is a compensable delay. In such cases, the courts or boards usually determine that when concurrent compensable and non-compensable delays occur, non-compensable delays take priority. This means that the contractor is granted a time extension with no additional compensation.

Using the same example, but with the strike ending on June 20, and the government ending the suspension on June 30, then the concurrent compensable and non-compensable delays are for different periods of time. In this case, the contractor is entitled to a 30-day time extension and also ten days of compensation. The contractor must, however, demonstrate the exact start and finish dates of the delays in order to receive compensation for the ten-day period during which the government was the sole delaying factor.

If the federal government suspended work on the project from June 1 through June 30 and the construction contractor experienced a strike from June 5 to June 30, the contractor may be entitled to a 30-day time extension *and* 30 days of compensation. This decision would be based on a concept known as the *primacy of delay*. The primacy of delay is established by determining which delay started first and which delay was controlling the project when the second delay occurred. Since the controlling delay in this case is the compensable delay, it takes priority over the non-compensable delay and the entire period is compensable. In the context of a critical path schedule, the 30-day suspension automatically gave every other activity in the network 30 additional days of extension, or *float*. All parties must carefully document the facts and dates surrounding these delays in order to receive time extensions and/or compensation.

Use of Schedules

The schedule that was in effect at the time that the alleged delay occurred is necessary in order to determine whether or not a contractor is entitled to a time extension. Without a detailed schedule, it is extremely difficult, if not impossible, to demonstrate that the contractor experienced a delay. Unfortunately, most construction contracts with the federal government are run using bar charts as opposed to Critical Path Method (CPM) schedules. With a typical bar chart, it is difficult for the government representative to ascertain whether the contractor has made an error in logic or in estimating his durations. (See Chapter 4 for a discussion on project schedules and illustrations of CPM and bar chart schedules.) With a detailed Critical Path Method schedule, it is far easier to ascertain who is at fault for the delay.

Requiring resource loading on the schedule makes it even easier for the government representative to determine the accuracy of the contractor's schedule. For instance, if a contractor's schedule shows that sheetrock will be installed on an entire floor of a building in three days with a crew of one foreman and two laborers, it is a relatively easy task for the government representative to calculate the productivity which that crew must demonstrate in order to meet that schedule.

An increasing number of federal agencies are requiring the use of CPM schedules for other construction projects. Perhaps the most notable agency that utilizes CPM is the Veterans Administration (VA). The VA requires detailed CPM schedules which are cost-and resource-loaded for all of their major construction projects. Corps of Engineers Districts are also now requiring the use of CPM schedules on complex projects.

Regardless of the government's contractual requirements for a schedule, the astute construction contractor will utilize CPM schedules on all of its projects with the government, since this type of schedule is the best basis from which all parties can assess and resolve a delay and its effects on a project.

Noncritical Delays

Noncritical delays involve activities which, if delayed, will not affect the overall duration of the project. These activities are known as having "float" time. Generally, the government's position is that a contractor is not entitled to compensation for a non critical delay. However, this is not always the case. If a contractor can demonstrate that an activity with float is delayed, and the delayed activity cost the contractor additional money, then the contractor has a right to request compensation.

For example, a contractor was required to construct a new hospital building and to rehabilitate two existing hospital buildings for the Veterans Administration. The contractor, in accordance with the contract, created a detailed Critical Path Method schedule for the project. The critical path for the project covered the construction of the new building and the rehabilitation of the two existing structures, and included 18 months of float. In other words, the activities could be delayed by as much as 18 months without exceeding the completion date for the project.

The contractor in the original schedule laid out an efficient sequence of work for the three structures in order to complete the project within the contract time requirements. Work on the two buildings to be rehabilitated was to be started at the inception of the project. The contractor was going to work the respective trade crews from one building to the next. Shortly after the beginning of the project, the Veterans Administration put a hold on all work on the two rehab buildings because of the need to make changes to the drawings and specifications. The hold on these buildings was in effect for almost 16 months. Although the suspension of work on these two buildings did not delay the overall completion of the project, it did seriously affect the *way* in which the work was performed, which increased the contractor's costs in the following ways.

The contractor's crew for drywall was originally scheduled under the proposed sequence to install drywall in the two rehab structures first and then in the new building. Because of the delay to the rehab structures, the drywall crews had to work in all three buildings simultaneously. This change had several increased cost impacts. First, the contractor required additional crews and, therefore, additional supervision which had not been included in the budget. Second, by increasing the size of the crew, the contractor did not benefit from the level of efficiency that would have occurred by maintaining one standard size crew. Working from one building to the next, the same crew would have overcome their initial learning curve and gained efficiency as they moved through the structures. Finally, during the 16-month delay, the labor rates for drywall crews increased and, therefore, the overall cost of drywall was higher than the budgeted amount. Since the suspension of work on the two rehab structures caused these escalated costs, the contractor was entitled to request compensation for this non critical delay. Although not warranting a time extension, the imposed delay did require that additional compensation be paid to the contractor.

Early Completion

A construction contractor has the right to complete a project early. In fact, the low bidder should be the contractor who has planned most efficiently to complete the project; a contractor saves money by saving time. Sometimes, however, a contractor plans to complete a project ahead of schedule, but is delayed by the government's action or lack of action. This is a difficult situation for the following reasons. The government may be reluctant to compensate the contractor for the delay since that delay did not affect the final completion date. The contractor, however, may have other commitments which are affected by his prolonged presence on the government project.

For example, a contractor receives a contract from the federal government to complete a project. The contract duration is specified as 300 calendar days from the date of the Notice to Proceed. The contractor plans on finishing this job in 200 calendar days. During the course of construction, the government makes several changes that delay the contractor's progress by 90 days. As a result, the contractor completes the project in 290 days. The contractor is clearly not entitled to a time extension since the contract completion date was not exceeded, but is entitled to compensation for the 90 day delay caused by the government's changes during the project.

In this case, it may be difficult to convince the government representative that the contractor is entitled to compensation for delay. The contractor must demonstrate with the project schedule that the project could have been completed early if not for the government delays. The government representative must review the contractor's schedule in detail, often meeting with the contractor to analyze the durations that indicate an overall project duration less than that specified in the contract documents, and to determine how those durations were calculated.

Contractors must realize that the schedule they are required to submit at the inception of the project should accurately reflect their plan for completing the project. For instance, if the contractor in the above example had originally planned to complete the job in 200 days, then the original schedule submission to the government should reflect the 200-day duration. Many contractors will submit a 300-day schedule to the government and then actually utilize a 200-day schedule in managing the project. Submitting an inaccurate schedule creates several problems. First, if the contractor has submitted a 300-day schedule, but is actually planning to complete the project early, a request for compensation due to a delay is viewed as questionable. Second, if the subcontractors are given the 200-day schedule, but find out that the government has been given a 300-day schedule, more problems result. Third, the federal government must know if the contractor is planning to complete early so that the pay schedule can be planned accordingly. If the government is not provided with the schedule duration that is actually intended, the funds to pay the contractor for the project may not be appropriated in time. In order to facilitate the government's fiscal management, the contractor should submit the early schedule.

The government representative should not reject a schedule merely because it promises a shorter duration for the project, but they should ensure that the contractor's estimate of time is reasonable. Early completion schedules should be monitored very closely throughout the duration of the project to prevent disputes arising over delays to the planned early completion date.

Delay Analysis

In order to determine what has occurred in the course of a time or scheduling problem, a delay analysis must be performed. This procedure is critically important in today's construction environment. A delay analysis is performed by comparing the contractor's "as-planned" schedule with the actual "as-built" information. This process sounds simple, but can be difficult to execute. The following example is used to illustrate the delay analysis.

A project was delayed 30 days and thus was completed 30 days beyond the specified contract completion date. No time extensions had been granted. The government and the contractor must sort out the reasons for the delays after the project is completed, and decide whether a time extension is warranted or if the contractor should be penalized for completing the project 30 days late.

The first step in delay analysis is to graphically illustrate the contractor's "as-planned" schedule, as shown in Figure 6.2. (Bar charts are used for both the as-planned and as-built schedules for this simple example. However, it is recommended that a detailed CPM format be used for all schedules submitted to the government at the beginning of the project.) This information should be extracted from the first approved schedule that the contractor submitted to the government. Whether this schedule is a Critical Path Method schedule or a bar chart, some determination must be made as to which activities were critical to the project completion. Critical activities are those which, if delayed, would delay the overall completion of the project.

Next, the "as-built" schedule — exactly what happened during the physical construction of the job — must be graphically defined, as shown in Figure 6.3. The analyst (the government representative or the contractor's personnel) can utilize daily reports or quality control/quality assurance reports to create an "as-built" schedule. A comparison is then made between the "as-planned" schedule and the "as-built" schedule as shown in Figure 6.4.

Merely looking at these two schedules can lead to erroneous conclusions. For example, Figure 6.4 shows that activity D was delayed by a period of 30 days. The government may contend that the reason activity D was delayed was because the general contractor did not mobilize the subcontractor to perform the work on time. The government may even refer to daily reports or quality control/quality assurance reports that back up this conclusion. While these conclusions may appear to be reasonable deductions, in reality they may be completely wrong. To perform an accurate delay analysis, the analyst should complete the "as-planned" schedule and the "as-built" schedule step-by-step, beginning with the first activity.

The "as-planned" and "as-built" schedules should be compared to determine the first delay that occurred to any of the critical activities. As shown in Figure 6.5, the first delay was a ten-day delay to activity A. Based on the "as-built" information, activity A took ten days longer to complete than was planned in the original schedule.

Before any further conclusions can be reached, the "as-planned" schedule must be adjusted to accommodate the first delay. An activity on the critical path of a project cannot begin until the

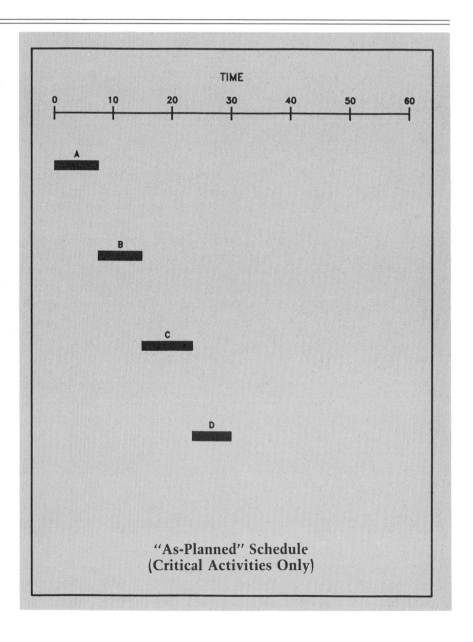

Figure 6.2

preceding activity is completed. Since activity A was delayed by ten days, activity B could not start until ten days later than was originally planned.

Figure 6.6 is the "as-planned" schedule showing activity A as originally planned, but with activities B, C, and D adjusted because of the initial delay to activity A. The "as-built" schedule is the same, since it depicts the historical facts showing when the activities were actually accomplished. The comparison of the *adjusted* "as-planned" activity B and the actual "as-planned" activity B shows that this activity also experienced a delay (a late start). In other words, although

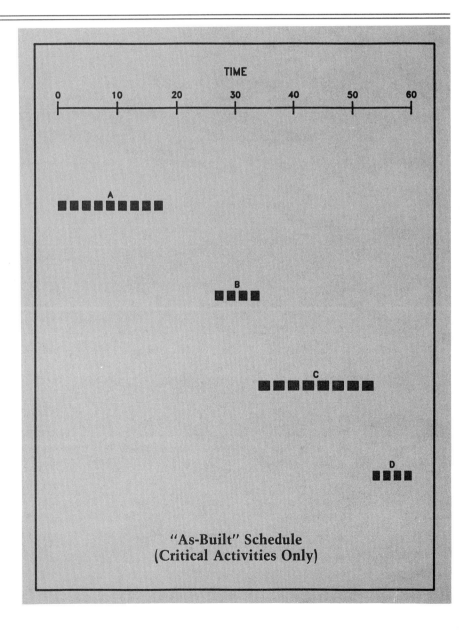

"As-Built" Schedule
(Critical Activities Only)

Figure 6.3

activity A was completed by a certain date and activity B *should* have begun immediately thereafter, activity B actually started ten days later. Now the second ten days of the delay to the schedule have been accounted for.

The next step in the process is to again adjust the "as-planned" schedule for the delay that occurred to activity B. Figure 6.7 shows the "as-planned" schedule with activities C and D adjusted for the delay to activity B. Figure 6.7 shows that activity C also experienced a delay. At first glance, the actual

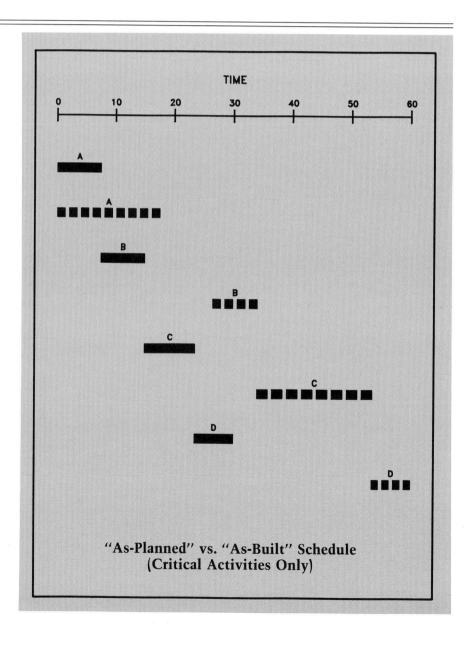

"As-Planned" vs. "As-Built" Schedule
(Critical Activities Only)

Figure 6.4

duration of activity C appears to have taken longer to accomplish than was planned. However, this too may be misleading.

All too often, the analyst identifies an initial start date and a completion date for an activity and connects those two points in time as one continuous activity. However, a thorough reading of the daily reports for each day during that time period may reveal that activity C was not performed continuously during that time frame. A more accurate representation of the "as-built" information for activity C is shown in Figure 6.8.

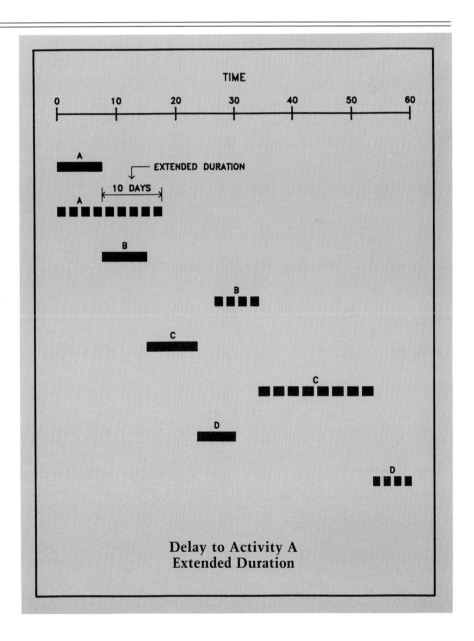

**Delay to Activity A
Extended Duration**

Figure 6.5

Figure 6.8 is identical to Figure 6.7 except that the "as-built" information in activity C has been more clearly defined to show what happened each day during that time frame. Figure 6.8 shows that activity C began, stopped for a period of five days, began again, and stopped again for a period of five days, began again, and then concluded on the final date. Activity C did not have an extended duration. This activity actually experienced two interruptions for a period of five days each, thus delaying activity C a total of ten days. As shown in this example, it is important to define the problem that occurs during the activity so that the analyst may draw accurate conclusions. Assuming

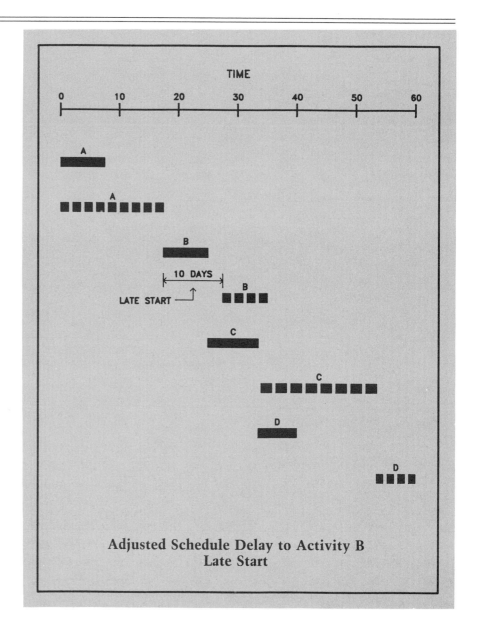

Adjusted Schedule Delay to Activity B
Late Start

Figure 6.6

that an activity simply has an extended duration may lead the analyst to conclude that the contractor did not work efficiently or that the government took too long if it was responsible for this activity. In reality, two separate interruptions occurred during that activity, each of which may have had a separate cause.

Now that the analysis has been performed on activity C, the "as-planned" schedule must be adjusted again. Figure 6.9 shows the adjustment for the delay that occurred to C. Activity D, "as-planned," has been bumped entirely because of the delays to activities A, B, and C. By comparing the planned duration of

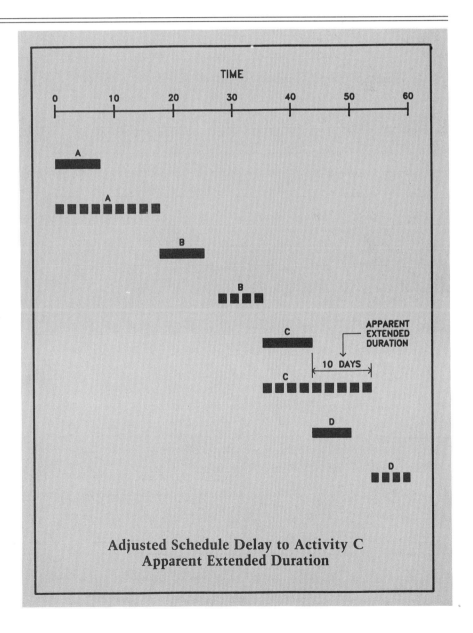

Adjusted Schedule Delay to Activity C
Apparent Extended Duration

Figure 6.7

activity D with the "as-built" activity D, it can be seen that no delay occurred during this activity. The delays occurred to the three preceding activities.

The analyst concludes that a 10-day delay occurred to activity A, a 10-day delay to activity B, and a 10-day delay to activity C. No delays occurred to activity D. The initial conclusions reached by simply looking at the comparison of the "as-planned" and "as-built" schedules were wrong.

Once the activities with delays have been identified, the analyst can ask the most important question: Were the delays caused by the contractor or the government? The analyst then makes a

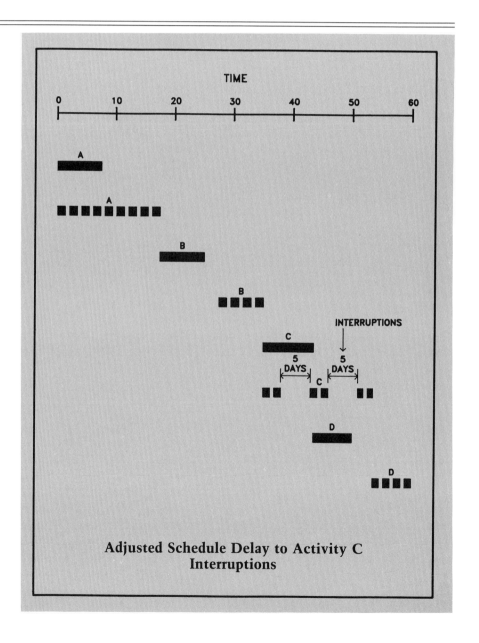

Adjusted Schedule Delay to Activity C Interruptions

Figure 6.8

determination as to the appropriateness of a time extension and/or the validity of the request for liquidated damages.

Although the preceding example was a simple one, the same procedure is used to analyze more complex situations.

Monitoring Delays During the Project

If the project is administered carefully by both the contractor and the government, delays will be identified as they occur. Staying up-to-date precludes the need for performing a delay analysis at the end of the project. Daily analyses should be compiled on a monthly basis and the schedule updated

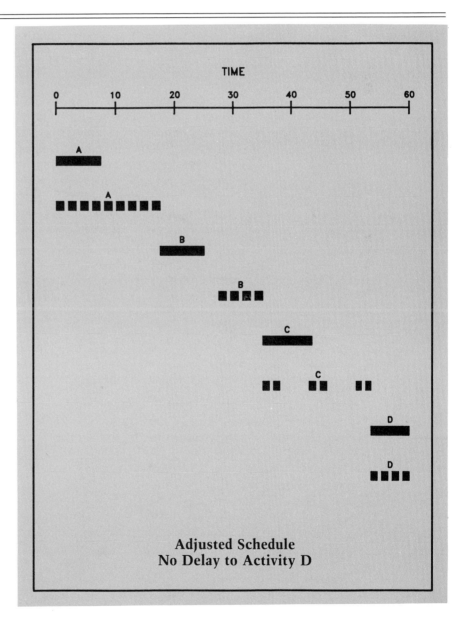

Figure 6.9

accordingly. If the project has a detailed CPM schedule, this kind of analysis can be performed using computerized files. In fact, this is standard practice with most CPM schedules. With each delay analysis, delays can be identified, their causes determined, and activities affected by the delays pinpointed. Then a decision can be made as to whether:

- A time extension is warranted
- The contractor can and should take steps to make up the time
- The government should be withholding money for liquidated damages

Not only critical, but also non critical activities can be delayed to the point that the project is delayed. For this reason, the analyst should consider both types of activities when comparing the as-planned and as-built schedules. For example, during the course of a delay analysis, the adjusted schedules may show a change or shift in the critical path because what was originally a non critical activity has now become critical. Again, a computerized CPM schedule will automatically account for this change in the normal calculation of the critical path.

When administering a construction contract, all parties should assess the schedule throughout the course of the project, preferably monthly. Performing a delay analysis at the end of the project is far more difficult and confusing and encourages many more disputes. The contractor should continually seek to identify when delays occurred to critical activities, and when changes occur to the critical path, and should respond appropriately by either asking for time extensions or accelerating work. If a time extension is not granted to the contractor, the government can direct him to finish, or accelerate the work, to meet the specified contract completion date.

To avoid such problems, it is important that the government resolve time extension questions immediately. By not resolving the question of time and/or not granting a valid time extension, the government may invite additional unwanted claims.

Chapter Seven
Pricing Changes

Pricing Changes

When presented with a request for a change, the contractor must supply the federal government with a price for that change. The contractor should supply this information as quickly as possible to establish the scope and cost of the change before any work is begun. Prompt attention to pricing helps to ensure that a formal change order is executed with an agreed upon price *before* the work is performed.

The change order cost estimate can be complicated, but it must be as accurate as possible. This chapter contains discussions of change order cost estimating, including how to estimate costs associated with time, overhead, and profit. Resolving prices *after* change work is performed is also discussed.

General Considerations

The government presents a *change order proposal* to the contractor. This proposal specifies the nature of the changed work, supplies any new drawings or revisions, and requests that the contractor supply a cost breakdown for the change order work. In response to the change order proposal, the contractor must submit a *cost and pricing proposal* to the federal government detailing the estimated cost of the work, including any additions or credits that may apply. If this procedure is followed, then an estimated cost is determined before any change order work begins. If this procedure is not followed, then the government may direct the contractor to do the work before the price is resolved. The construction contract clearly states that the government has the right to give this directive. However, fewer disputes arise if the cost can be established and a formal change order executed before the work is performed.

Familiarity with Government Contracts
In pricing change orders, the contractor should be intimately familiar with the requirements of the construction contract. Specifically, certain costs are allowable, others are not. For instance, if a contractor is doing work for the Corps of Engineers, equipment expenses are paid based on designated rates published by the Corps of Engineers in an equipment cost guide (normalized to specific District Offices throughout the

country). Similarly, there may be a specified mark-up for overhead for extra work. The contractor must comply with this specified mark-up and any other requirements specific to the government agency involved.

Certification of Accuracy

If the cost of a change or extra work exceeds the designated dollar amounts, the government may require a certification of the accuracy of the cost and pricing data. For construction contracts with the government, this limit is presently $100,000. When the dollar amount for the changes reaches this limit, the contractor must certify that the cost and pricing data is accurate and the government must perform an audit of the accuracy of these costs.

The contractor should be aware that the government has the right (according to the contract) to audit any costs regardless of the dollar amount. However, audits are generally not performed until the specified cost levels for the work have been met.

Cost and Pricing Proposals

A contractor submits a cost and pricing proposal for extra work with a detailed breakdown of all the elements involved in that change, including any cost for subcontractors and suppliers. Subcontractors and suppliers, likewise, must include in their cost estimates a detailed breakdown of their final price. The detailed breakdowns should include labor, materials, equipment, fringe benefits, and overhead. Refer to Figure 7.1 for a sample Contract Modification Proposal and Acceptance.

The contractor should be prepared to meet with the government representative to discuss and perhaps justify all of the items in the cost proposal. The government is required to review the cost and pricing proposal provided by the contractor and to enter into negotiations with the contractor prior to approving the amount on a formal change order.

Costs Associated with Time

Probably the most difficult type of change to estimate is a cost that relates to time (costs associated with a delay to the construction project). As discussed in Chapter 6, costs associated with time are only compensable to a contractor when the delay is caused by the government. The contractor's methods for pricing time-related costs is discussed in the following sections.

When a delay is determined to be compensable because the completion time of a project was extended by government action or inaction, the contractor must estimate the cost for the delay. Typical costs incurred because of delays are listed below.

- Extended Field Overhead
- Escalation of Labor
- Idle Equipment Cost
- Escalation of Materials
- Unabsorbed Home Office Overhead

Figure 7.2 is an example of a submission by a contractor for delay costs associated with a change on a project. In this case, a contractor has requested costs for escalation of labor, extended

CONTRACT MODIFICATION PROPOSAL AND ACCEPTANCE
(Modification of less than $25,000)
For use of this form, see ER 1180-1-1.

1. ISSUING OFFICE	2. CONTRACT NO.	3. MODIFICATION NO.
U.S. Army Engineer District	DACA	P00005 (85-17-F)

4. TO (Contractor)	5. PROJECT LOCATION AND DESCRIPTION
	Hydrant Refueling

6. *A proposal is requested for making the hereinafter described change in accordance with specification and drawing revisions cited herein or listed in attachment hereto. Submit your proposal in space indicated on page 2, attach detailed breakdown of prime and subcontract costs. (See the clause of this contract entitled, "Modification Proposals - Price Breakdown") DO NOT start work under this proposed change until you receive a copy signed by the Contracting Officer or a directive to proceed.*

Date	Typed Name and Title	Signature

7. DESCRIPTION OF CHANGE: *Pursuant to the clause of this contract entitled, "Changes", the contractor shall furnish all plant labor and material, and perform all work necessary to accomplish the following described work:*

MODIFICATION NAME: Remove Additional Unsuitable Material

Remove unsuitable material in new apron paving lane 2 in vicinity of Station 400, and replace this material with satisfactory fill compacted to contract requirements.

CHANGES TO THE CONTRACT DRAWINGS SHALL BE AS FOLLOWS: None

CHANGES TO THE CONTRACT SPECIFICATIONS SHALL BE AS FOLLOWS: None

CHANGES TO THE PAYMENT (BIDDING) SCHEDULE SHALL BE AS FOLLOWS: Add item P00005, MCB 85-17-F, "Remove Additional Unsuitable Material", Job L. S. $826.00.

CHANGES TO THE NETWORK ANALYSIS SYSTEM SHALL BE AS FOLLOWS: Increase the amount and time of Activity 470-471 by $826.00 and one (1) day, respectively.

CHANGE IN THE CONTRACT PRICE: The contract consideration covering all costs related to this modification is hereby increased by the sum of EIGHT HUNDRED TWENTY-SIX AND 00/100 ($826.00) DOLLARS.

CHANGE IN THE CONTRACT TIME: The time for completion of performance under said contract is hereby extended one (1) calendar day.

It is further understood and agreed that this adjustment constitutes compensation in full on behalf of the contractor and its subcontractors and suppliers for all costs and markup directly or indirectly attributable to the change ordered, for all delays related thereto, and for performance of the change within the time frame stated.

Except as hereby Modified, all terms and conditions of said contract as heretofore Modified remain unchanged and in full force and effect.

The foregoing modification is hereby accepted: CONTRACTOR	UNITED STATES OF AMERICA
BY_____ Signature	_____ Signature
Date — Typed Name and Title	Date — Typed Name and Title

ENG FORM 3938
1 JUN 77   EDITION OF SEP 70 IS OBSOLETE.   ☆U.S. Government Printing Office: 1979—625-566   **PAGE 1 OF 2 PAGES**

Figure 7.1

field overhead, idle equipment, and for unabsorbed home office overhead. The contractor has also requested costs for additional bond premiums and for profit.

Field Office Overhead

Extended field overhead involves a calculation by the contractor of those items that are directly associated with maintaining the field office. As can be seen in Figure 7.1, field office overhead includes the cost of the superintendent, job trailer, utilities, the superintendent's truck, and the portable toilet. The contractor can demonstrate the total cost for these items by multiplying the daily costs by 30 (days). This calculation is straightforward since it involves tangible items which are obvious to anyone

Contractor Delay Costs		
Extended Field Overhead:		
30-day delay		
Superintendent @ $200/day		$ 6,000.00
Trailer @ $10.20/day		306.00
Utilities @ $7.65/day		229.50
Temporary Toilet @ $4.20/day		126.00
Truck @ $8.00/day		240.00
	Subtotal	$ 6,901.50
Unabsorbed Home Office Overhead:		
See calculations in Figure 2		$10,241.10
	Subtotal	$17,142.60
Escalation of Labor:		
220 man-hours @ $.50		$ 110.00
	Subtotal	$17,252.60
Idle Equipment:		
Backhoe – 84 hours @ $31.50		$ 2,646.00
Dozer – 82 hours @ $43.20		$ 3,542.40
	Subtotal	$23,441.00
Bond:		
0.005 x $23,441.00		$ 117.20
	Subtotal	$23,558.20
Profit:		
10% x $23,558.20		$ 2,355.82
	Subtotal	$25,914.02

Figure 7.2

who inspects the site. Both the government and the contractor should keep records to verify that these items were on site during the delay period.

Labor

A request for compensation for escalated labor costs should include the exact number of labor hours that were moved into a more expensive time frame because of the delay. In the example in Figure 7.1, the contractor has asserted that 220 man-hours of carpenters' time was moved into a time frame where the carpenters' rate increased by $.50 an hour. Therefore, the contractor's compensation is $.50 an hour multiplied by 220 man-hours. Figure 7.3 is another example of how to determine the labor cost of a delay. In this case, the contractor was using union labor. An existing trade agreement was to increase the rates for laborers from $11 an hour to $12 an hour, starting on a certain date. A two-week delay was then caused by the government early in the project. Because of the delay, the contractor was granted a time extension for two additional weeks. Now the contractor and the government are attempting to resolve the extra direct labor costs associated with this two-week delay.

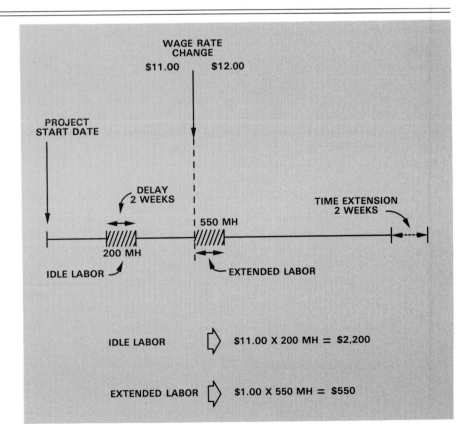

Figure 7.3

During the period of the actual delay, the contractor is asserting that manpower was sitting idle, waiting for the government to make a decision. In Figure 7.2, this is noted as 200 man-hours of idle labor.

The contractor is requesting $2,200 ($11 an hour multiplied by 200 man-hours). The contractor must demonstrate that nothing could be done to mitigate these costs. The government may question why the manpower could not have been utilized elsewhere on the project, on another project, or sent back to the union hall. If the contractor was committed to using this labor and could not reasonably use it elsewhere, then he is entitled to the additional $2,200 for the idle labor.

The contractor is also claiming that because of the delay, it has experienced extended labor, or labor working in a more expensive time frame. This is often termed *escalation of labor*, but for simplicity the more common term of *extended labor* is used. Because the crews were working in the time frame in which the labor cost went up to $12, the contractor is requesting an additional $3,600. However, the contractor is not entitled to $3,600. Some may argue that the contractor is entitled at least to $300, or 300 hours multiplied by the additional $1 an hour. In reality, both conclusions are wrong, and are based on a lack of understanding of the impact to labor caused by a delay.

The *true* impact of the delay is determined by an analysis of the certified payrolls for that two-week period of time. The payrolls show that the contractor's labor force actually worked 550 man-hours during those two weeks. Therefore, the contractor is entitled to $1 an hour multiplied by the 550 man-hours that were worked in the more expensive time frame. The final resolution of this situation is shown in Figure 7.4.

In any delay, the analyst should step back and ask — How was the contractor impacted? Exactly how did the delay affect his operations? Did he experience increased or decreased costs? The same approach that was used for labor can be applied to equipment and materials.

Equipment
While a contractor may not use extra equipment costs for extra work, extra storage and rental charges may be incurred if equipment stands idle on the site during the period of the delay. In the example, the idle equipment item includes a backhoe and a bulldozer which, because of the delay, had to remain on the site for 30 days longer than expected.

Unabsorbed Home Office Overhead
The unabsorbed home office overhead is perhaps the most difficult concept to understand in estimating delay damages. Basically, unabsorbed home office overhead means that because of a delay to a project, a contractor is unable to take on additional work and, therefore, cannot prorate the home office overhead cost to a new project.

Contractors charge a fixed percentage of the home office cost to each project. If a project is delayed, then that project takes on a larger share of the home office cost. This, in turn, forces the other projects to absorb more than their percentage of the home office costs. While this concept may be difficult to understand, it is generally recognized and accepted by the government. Numerous decisions have been made by the boards and courts substantiating the validity of the request for the unabsorbed home office cost.

Eichleay Formula

The calculation of unabsorbed home office overhead cost in federal contracts is based on a formula known as the *Eichleay Formula*. This formula originated from a decision before the Armed Services Board of Contract Appeals in 1960. It is a straightforward three-step formula for calculating the pro rata portion of the home office overhead cost attributable to this particular project (see Figure 7.5). The formula provides a daily unabsorbed home office overhead rate which is then multiplied by the number of days in the compensable delay.

Some particular requirements of the Eichleay Formula should be noted. The total contract billings, total company billings, and the total home office overhead are calculated for the entire

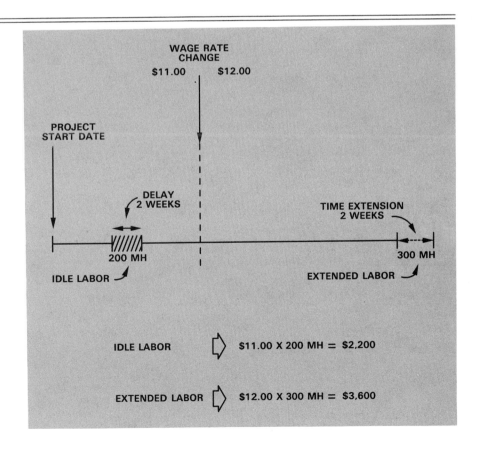

Figure 7.4

period of the contract, including the delay. The total contract time also includes the delay period. The calculations are on a calendar day basis.

There have been numerous decisions by the boards and courts concerning the use of the Eichleay Formula for calculating unabsorbed home office overhead. As long as it can be demonstrated to the government that because of the delay the contractor was precluded from bidding other work due to a limited bonding capacity, the Eichleay Formula is accepted by the government as a reasonable estimate of compensation for unabsorbed home office costs during a delay. For this reason, other projects upon which the contractor was unable to bid should be documented.

In the delay calculation in Figure 7.4, the contractor has requested additional profit. If the requested delay costs relate back to the Suspension of Work Clause in the contract, the Suspension of Work Clause specifically precludes compensation for such additional profit. (See Chapter 6 for a description of this clause.) However, if the delay was occasioned by a change under the Changes Clause or by a differing site condition under that clause, then the contractor is entitled to compensation for profit.

Unabsorbed Home Office Overhead
Eichleay Formula

1. $\dfrac{\text{Total Contract Billings}}{\text{Total Company Billings}}$ x Total Home Office Overhead = Allocable Overhead

$\dfrac{\$3,273,654}{\$37,461,956}$ x $\$1,765,723 = \$154,299$

2. $\dfrac{\text{Allocable Overhead}}{\substack{\text{Total Contract Time} \\ \text{(Including Delay)}}}$ = Daily Overhead

$\dfrac{\$154,299}{452 \text{ Days}} = \$341.37$ per day

3. Daily Overhead x Days of Compensable Delay = Total Unabsorbed Home Office Overhead

$\$341.37/\text{day}$ x 30 days = $\$10,241.10$

Figure 7.5

The Government Estimate and Negotiation

Before the government can agree to the cost of a change, it must create its own estimate of the cost of the change. In some cases, the government accepts the contractor's estimate and adopts it as the government estimate. However, properly administered change orders have a separate government estimate performed either by their site staff or by support staff in the government office. Normally, the contractor is not privy to the government estimate for a change order. However, if the government's estimate is not at least the amount of the change requested by the contractor, the price must be negotiated. The government usually negotiates with the contractor on each change order.

The government provides the contractor with forms to initiate the change, but may not always provide all of the associated back-up documentation. However, the government's own paperwork should include records of negotiations with the contractor and should justify the agreed upon price. After the change is executed, the contractor can request copies of this documentation under the Freedom of Information Act.

Resolving Prices After Work is Performed

Unfortunately, many change order prices are resolved after the work is performed. The government may contend that it takes too long for the paperwork to be processed and that the work has to be performed immediately. Contractors may also contribute to the problem by taking more time than necessary in submitting cost proposals to the government. Most of the time, change order prices could actually be resolved upfront. To do so requires a concerted effort and diligence on the part of both the government and the contractor. To avoid disputes, both parties should work to resolve the change costs before the work is performed.

Cost Records

When a change order is being negotiated after the work has been performed, the contractor should be prepared to substantiate (with documentation) all the costs that were incurred for the change. This means that the contractor must keep detailed records of all labor, materials, and equipment costs incurred in the course of performing the extra work. Contractors should utilize a standard and distinctive form of documentation for recording the costs associated with changes.

For example, a contractor performing change order work may use a *pink* time sheet for the labor report as opposed to the *white* time sheet usually used. This is helpful for two reasons. First, it is much easier to pull time sheets that are pink from a stack of the white time sheets than to sort through a pile of white sheets, looking for those that pertain to the change order. Second, most of the time, field personnel record the labor, equipment, and materials information. Chances are, they will pay particular attention to the change form since it is pink, and will, hopefully, be reminded that they must record as much information as possible.

When the government directs the contractor to do the work before a price is established, the contractor performs the work, tracks the costs, and then submits those costs to the government for compensation. The government, upon reviewing these costs, may contend that the charges are too high. If the contractor contends that these are actual costs, the situation must be resolved through the disputes process, if neither party is willing to compromise. The disputes process is described in Chapters 10 and 11.

Profit from Changes

One final point should be made concerning costs and changes. The government has very clearly defined rules concerning which costs are allowed and which are not. For example, calculating the cost of unabsorbed home office overhead (using the Eichleay Formula) some of the generally accepted costs which a contractor may normally report may not be allowed by the government. For a complete discussion of allowable costs, the reader is referred to the *Federal Acquisition Regulation*.

The assertion is often made by government personnel that contractors "low bid" projects, planning to make their money on the changes that will occur. The fact is that the majority of contractors do not "low bid" jobs based on this premise, because this is not a safe approach to making a profit. It could, in fact, be disastrous. A contractor who approaches a project on the presumption that all profits will be made on changes is gambling. Most changes are not resolved immediately. Furthermore, on most changes, prices are negotiated downward. A "gambler" who is trying to profit on changes is usually forced to finance the changes and may, in the final resolution, recover only a portion of the costs involved.

Contractors should not approach a government construction project with a low bid, assuming that profits will be made on the changes. Most experienced contractors attest that the most profitable jobs and the most efficient projects are those that have the *fewest changes*. In general, changes are disruptive and time consuming, and in many cases, the contractor may feel inadequately compensated.

Summary

The contractor's cost and pricing proposal for changes may not always be accepted by the government. Often, the government produces its own cost estimate to be compared with that of the contractor. If the contractor's price is higher than the government's estimate, then two courses of action may be taken. The government may perform an audit of the contractor's price. (See Chapter 8 for more about audits.) With or without an audit, the government may enter into negotiations with the contractor. Guidelines for negotiating with the government are presented in Chapter 9. If negotiations prove unsuccessful, the contractor may initiate the disputes procedure, explained in Chapters 10 and 11.

Chapter Eight
Government Audits

Chapter Eight
Government Audits

Contractors who deal with federal agencies should be aware of the fraud-conscious atmosphere in which all federal agencies now operate. Although it has always been illegal to submit false or fraudulent claims, there has never been a time where the scrutiny of change orders, settlements, and claims has been so intensive. For this reason, contractors must take care to avoid even the appearance of impropriety. All requests for additional compensation should be supported with carefully compiled cost and pricing data, to satisfy the scrutiny of a government audit. The proper procedures for a government audit are described in this Chapter. The standard government audit clause, found in the Federal Acquisition Regulation [FAR 52.214-26], is shown in Figure 8.1.

The contractor is required to make the materials identified in the audit clause available at its offices at "reasonable times" for examination, audit, or reproduction. These materials are to be retained for three years after final payment under the contract, or any other period specified in Subpart 4.7 of the FAR (Contractor Records Retention).

Contractors should anticipate an audit whenever a modification to the contract is executed in excess of $500,000, and for lesser amounts as determined by the Contracting Officer. If a claim in excess of $500,000 has been filed, an audit is often performed as a prerequisite to negotiations. Contractors should be aware that the agency may be seeking to delay the negotiations by waiting for the audit (an audit can take six months to one year to complete). When the merits of the claim are in dispute, the contractor should insist that negotiations and discussions on the merits proceed, with the understanding that any settlement will be subject to the results of the audit. If the government does not agree that the contractor is entitled to additional compensation, the audit results become irrelevant.

Preparing for the Audit

Record Keeping
Many contractors have rather "loose" record keeping practices. This "loose" approach can be fatal if a request for additional

compensation is challenged by a federal agency. Careful records must be kept to document costs which will eventually be included in requests for additional compensation. These records should include cancelled checks, invoices, payroll records, financial statements, and all accounting records which verify overhead and equipment rates. It is most helpful to have an accountant familiar with government cost accounting check and ensure that the costs requested are allowable under applicable government regulations.

Allowable Costs

In auditing a contractor's cost records, the government is guided by regulations which determine allowable costs. Allowable costs are defined in the Federal Acquisition Regulation (FAR) as costs that are reasonable and chargeable to the contract. Although this is a broad definition, FAR Section 31 specifically explains the cost principles of the government, listing many types of costs that a contractor may incur. These cost principles apply to both cost-reimbursable and fixed-price contracts. When applied to fixed-price contracts, these principles primarily govern extended overhead calculations and the negotiation of changes over $100,000 in value.

Reasonable Costs

To be allowed, costs must be deemed reasonable. To be reasonable, the cost must:

Standard Government Audit Clause
Audit-Sealed Bidding (April 1985)

a. Cost or pricing data. If the Contractor has submitted cost or pricing date in connection with the pricing of any modification to this contract, unless the pricing was based on adequate price competition, established catalog or market prices of commercial items sold in substantial quantities to the general public, or prices set by law or regulation, the Contracting Officer or a representative who is an employee of the Government shall have the right to examine and audit all books, records, documents, and other data of the Contractor (including computations and projections) related to negotiating, pricing or performing the modification, in order to evaluate the accuracy, completeness, and currency of the cost or pricing data. In this case of pricing any modification, the Comptroller General of the United States or a representative who is an employee of the Government shall have the same rights . . .

Figure 8.1

- be generally recognized as an ordinary or necessary part of the business
- follow sound business practices
- comply with federal, state, and local laws
- be consistent with the contractor's established practices

Every situation is different; therefore, the determination of reasonableness is made by examining all of the facts and circumstances surrounding each cost.

Chargeability to the Contract

Costs must be chargeable to the contract if they are to be allowed. Chargeability involves determining whether or not the cost can be allocated to the contract. To be chargeable to the contract, the cost must:

- be specifically incurred during the contract administration
- benefit the contract and other work
- be necessary for the overall operation of the business

If a cost is reasonable and chargeable to the contract, it will be allowable, unless specifically prohibited by the cost regulations.

Unallowable Costs

There are specific unallowable costs determined by the government. These are listed in the Federal Acquisition Regulation (FAR). The following costs are considered unallowable, as noted in the FAR, Section 31:

- bad debts
- interest
- entertainment
- contributions or donations
- fines and penalties
- lobbying
- losses on other contracts
- alcoholic beverages
- business organization costs (incorporation, reorganization, merger)

Other Costs

There are a number of other costs which may or may not be allowable depending on the circumstances surrounding the cost. Examples of these costs, which are described in FAR Section 31, include:

- training
- depreciation
- insurance
- employee morale, health, welfare (generally allowable)

These issues require guidance from a professional who is familiar with the aforementioned cost principles, the FAR, and judicial rulings on allowability.

If an auditor raises questions about a specific cost, the contractor should be prepared to offer as much background and explanation as possible to support the reasonableness of the cost and why it must be charged to this contract. The government will not consider any argument to include unallowable costs.

Cost Principles

The cost principles in FAR Section 31 apply to construction contracts whenever the contractor submits cost or pricing data in support of a proposal, modification, or change order which will be negotiated under the contract. For the purpose of contract modifications, these principles are applied by the government on any proposal over $100,000. All proposals over $500,000 require an audit to be performed; the government's auditors will use these cost principles in evaluating contractor's costs.

Home Office Overhead

Another area governed by these cost principles concerns any request for extended home office overhead during government-caused delays. These operating costs are evaluated in order to determine an allowable overhead rate. (See Chapter 7, "Pricing Changes," for more information about compensation for extended home office overhead.)

Certification

The Department of Defense now requires that contractors certify that there are no unallowable costs in their requests for overhead payments. A senior corporate official must sign the certification (under penalty of perjury) and indicate that the claim for overhead costs does not contain any unallowable costs. This certification is required only for Department of Defense contracts, and then only for *cost contracts*, not *fixed price construction contracts*. The contractor need only be concerned with overhead certification for cost-reimbursement construction contracts with a Department of Defense agency (Army, Navy, or Air Force).

This certification is required in addition to the certification required by the Contract Disputes Act (See Chapter 11).

The Audit Procedure

The audit function of the government is accomplished through two principal sources: *in-house auditors*, and the staff of the *Defense Contract Audit Agency* (DCAA). The latter group is available for any Department of Defense contract or agency at the request of the Contracting Officer.

The general audit procedure begins with the Contracting Officer's written request to the auditor, accompanied by the contractor's cost proposal, cost or pricing data (Standard Form 1411 — see Chapter 3, Figure 3.7), if applicable, and a technical report by the agency on the matter. With this information, the auditor visits the contractor's home office to begin the actual audit.

The extent of the audit depends upon its purpose. If the matter relates to home office overhead, the auditor will review financial statements, operating costs, and the accounting system. If material prices are involved, he will review invoice payments for material and other accounting records. For equipment rates, the auditor may wish to review purchase documents, lease agreements, usage costs, fuel records, repair records, etc.

The auditor will review these records at the contractor's office, and compile a set of *working papers* which contain his calculations and notes. From these working papers, he will develop the final audit report. This typewritten report records the auditor's analysis of the proposal or claim, and makes recommendations to the Contracting Officer regarding the proposed costs and their adequacy for negotiation purposes. The Defense Contract Audit Agency indicates, in each report, that the audit report may be released to the contractor at the discretion of the Contracting Officer. However, this report may not be released to the public under the Freedom of Information Act.

The audit report usually contains a breakdown of the contractor's costs as follows: *costs questioned; costs unsupported;* or *costs unresolved.* If a cost is questioned, it may be unallowable by the contract, regulation, or statute; not in accordance with generally accepted accounting principles; or questioned by the engineering or technical report. If a cost is unsupported, it lacks sufficient evidence for the auditor to make a conclusion about the cost. A cost that is unresolved is one that has not been audited. Explanatory notes may accompany the cost breakdowns.

Summary

The audit report is made available to the Contracting Officer and may become a very important document during negotiations, particularly if the auditor concludes that the contractor's costs are not adequately supported, or are questionable. However, audit reports are *advisory only;* the Contracting Officer has the authority to accept or reject the auditor's recommendations.

Some auditors may be overzealous advocates of the agency's position and attempt to list as many cost items as possible as "questioned" or "unsupported." It is important, therefore, to request a copy of the audit report so that the contractor can rebut the auditor's statements during negotiations.

If the contractor's request for additional compensation is not resolved through *negotiations* (see Chapter 9), the matter may ultimately be decided by a judge through the *disputes process.* If an entitlement decision is favorable and the board or court agrees to hear testimony about costs, the contractor's attorney will have the opportunity to cross-examine government witnesses, including the auditor who disagrees with the claim. The contractor, in a court or board hearing, must demonstrate that its costs were actually incurred and that they were reasonable. The disputes process is discussed in Chapters 10 and 11.

Chapter Nine
Negotiations

Chapter Nine
Negotiations

In construction contracting with the federal government, negotiating is an art, not a science. There are many occasions where the contractor must negotiate with government representatives to reach an agreement on various aspects of the contract. This chapter covers some of the more common circumstances for negotiation and offers some background and suggestions for the negotiating parties.

Negotiating can be defined as *discussion*, or *communication* between two parties for the purpose of reaching an agreement or settlement on a particular issue. It is generally agreed that negotiation is the "cheapest way to go" in resolving differences that may arise during the course of a construction contract.

Opportunities for Negotiation

Award of Contract

There are many different types of negotiation that may take place in the course of construction contracting with the government. Almost all construction contracts with the government are competitively bid. There is, therefore, no negotiation process at this stage since the government simply awards the contract to the lowest responsive and responsible bidder (as identified in a "sealed bid"). However, in some instances, the government may award construction contracts through the vehicle of a *negotiated procurement* ("competitive proposal"). In these cases, the parties involved must be able to negotiate effectively. Designers and consultants who work for the federal government are generally awarded contracts through this negotiated procurement method. For these entities, negotiating skills are extremely important at the contract stage.

The Construction Phase

During the course of construction, there are many opportunities for negotiation. The first may arise at the pre-construction meeting. At this point, the contractor or the government may wish to negotiate the method or sequence in which the work is to be performed. It is not uncommon for either party to make suggestions during a pre-construction meeting, in order to clarify the contract documents. These suggestions may require some negotiation to reach a consensus as to how the contract will be executed.

Throughout the course of construction, any questions concerning changes will be the subject of a negotiation session. The government is required to negotiate every change order and must, in fact, make a formal record of this negotiation on the change order form. Negotiations will also be conducted to resolve questions of contract performance, claims or disputes, and even terminations.

When the parties are negotiating a change order, two issues are involved: price or *cost*, and *time*, if the change requires that additional time be added to the contract. (See Chapter 5 for a more complete explanation of change orders to government contracts.)

Location of Negotiation Meetings

Negotiation meetings between contractor and government representatives normally take place at the government offices. In some cases, the government may have a full time staff and office at the project. More often, meetings will take place at the offices of the agency through which the contract is being performed. There are several reasons why these meetings are held at the government offices:

- Government representatives may feel that there is a psychological advantage in having the contractor come to their offices.
- Government employee travel time and costs are kept to a minimum.
- The government representative has access to all government resources, such as technical or legal expertise, which may be required during the course of the negotiations.
- The contracting officer or higher authority responsible for the contract is available at that government office and can be consulted should an impasse occur during the course of the negotiations.

If negotiations are held at government offices, a separate room should be available to the contractor for private discussions which generally occur during breaks in the session. Regardless of the location of the negotiation, all parties involved should make sure that they are not interrupted during the session. Frequent interruptions or the intermittent loss of one or more participants breaks the continuity of the negotiation process and may impede the rapid resolution of the problem.

Levels of Negotiation

In negotiating with the federal government for items such as a change order on a construction contract, the contractor generally conducts the initial negotiation at the field level. Initial negotiations may be conducted with the contracting officer's representative, who is on the site handling the project. It must be remembered that the dollar value of the change is crucial.

The contractor should also insure that the government representative conducting the negotiation has the authority to reach an agreement. One of the dangers in negotiating with the government is a misunderstanding of levels of authority. The only persons who can bind the government are the Contracting Officer and his *authorized* representatives. The contractor must assess the authority of the government's representatives at the negotiation. Representatives who do not have the authority to bind the government can only make a recommendation to the Contracting Officer regarding the settlement. Even the government's trial attorney handling the dispute does not have binding authority. Generally, the Contracting Officer endorses such recommendations and the settlement becomes binding.

If negotiations are required beyond the field level, the contractor meets with personnel from an area, district, or regional office of the agency. If the negotiations become significant enough, the session may be taken to a higher level, to include the Contracting Officer. Government representatives may consider it their responsibility to shield the Contracting Officer from involvement in time consuming sessions. Nevertheless, if agreement cannot be reached, the contractor should firmly request his right to meet with the Contracting Officer to negotiate a resolution to the problem.

In some instances, negotiations may be taken to an authority at a higher level than that of the Contracting Officer. For example, if a contractor is working on a construction project for the Corps of Engineers, the Contracting Officer may be the District Engineer. Above the District Engineer would be the Division Engineer and the Division Staff. Technically, the Division Engineer and the Division Staff cannot make agreements with the contractor on behalf of the government with the contractor since the Contracting Officer has the official responsibility for these issues. However, in some instances, the higher authority can add a different perspective which may well increase the chances of reaching an agreement.

The contractor should not be afraid to elevate the discussions throughout the process, particularly if there is a stalemate at the lower levels. All too often, government representatives at the lower levels may be so involved with the project that they lack the objectivity to reach a rational agreement.

Preparation

The most important part of a successful negotiation is the preparation process. The parties cannot reasonably reach an agreement that is fair to both if they are not prepared when they enter the session. The preparation process has several facets. First, both parties should meticulously review all the documents surrounding the issue to be discussed. These documents include not only the Request for Proposal (which the government may send to the contractor) and the contractor's proposal, but also all other existing information concerning the issue to be negotiated. This collection may include quality control/quality assurance reports, daily logs, diaries, submittal logs, specifications, and drawings. Both parties should review all reports associated with the contract, particularly in terms of quality and time. The time aspect is addressed by progress reports, photographs, and the schedules that exist on the job. Although these items may not be appropriate to every change order, in cases where they are required, they must be reviewed and understood.

Documentation

Both parties should review the relevant documents, identifying which are significant to the discussion and preparing copies to have available during the course of discussion. If the contractor is going to be attending a meeting at a government office, he should bring all of the appropriate documentation. The government representatives should have their documentation readily available at their offices.

Analysis

During the preparation phase, both parties must analyze the issue and prepare their respective positions. Such analysis should address the issue of *costs* — specifically whether or not the costs being requested are fully justified and supported. The analysis should also address *time*. The contractor must consider whether the change or the situation has caused a delay to the project that necessitates a time extension to the contract. If there is a delay, the contractor must be fully prepared to demonstrate to the government in a very clear and convincing manner how the project was delayed, the magnitude of the delay, and the justification for the time extension.

The analysis must address not only the technical issues, but also the legal ramifications of the change. Prior to a negotiation session, both parties should consult with counsel and obtain an opinion as to the legality of the positions they plan to take during the negotiation session.

Legal Counsel

In some circumstances, the contractor or the government representative may want to have counsel present at the negotiation session. This is perfectly acceptable. However, if one side has counsel present, then it is in the best interest of the other side to also have counsel present. If either party intends to bring their lawyer to the session, they should notify the other side well in advance that this will be the case. In this way, both can prepare and schedule accordingly. The decision to have counsel present in a negotiation session depends solely on the issue to be discussed, the legal ramifications of that issue, and the overall significance and cost of the issue.

Strategy

Both parties should have defined their strategy before the negotiating session. They should define for themselves clear-cut objectives that they feel they must attain during the session. The next step is to decide:

- which objectives must not be compromised under any circumstances
- which objectives can be compromised and what is expected in return
- which objectives are desirable, but not essential, and can be traded without getting very much in return

Another strategy issue involves assessing the positions that the other side may take during the session. Such an assessment helps to avoid surprises during the negotiations. In defining positions for the negotiating session, both parties should consider the following factors:

- the contractor's desire to perform the work
- any pressures on the government in terms of time or political considerations
- any regulatory pressures that affect either party
- the legal ramifications of the issues

While the initial focus of the negotiation may be on the cost of the settlement, other elements should also be considered. For example, removal of an unsatisfactory performance rating, acceptance of in-place work that does not strictly conform to the specifications, substitution of equipment or materials, time extensions, or remission of liquidated damages. Once the goals or objectives are established, the strategy for negotiations can be planned. All those attending the negotiations should understand which points can be conceded and which points are firm.

Persons Attending Negotiations

Another important strategy is the selection of participants in the negotiations. A negotiating team should be made up of key employees who have the factual knowledge to back up the contractor's position. Be aware, however, that a large number of people at the negotiating session can present certain problems. The government representatives may attempt to engage these people in extensive questioning, which could undermine the contractor's position. Another hazard is that the negotiations may stray from the objectives. On the other hand, the *right people* must be present to support the contractor's position. Above all, one person with authority must be in charge of the negotiations and settlement at the meeting.

Provide Information in Advance

Further strategy involves determining how much information should be provided to the other side before the negotiation session. Many people believe that it is best to go to a negotiation session without having provided the other side with any advance notice of their position. This approach may actually be counterproductive, as it lengthens the overall negotiation process and, to some extent, tends to alienate the other side. Generally, it is most productive to provide the other side with as much information as possible prior to the negotiation session. If the other party is properly informed, they cannot say, "Well, we understand what you are saying, but now we need time to evaluate it." Good information exchange precludes the use of such delaying tactics.

Remain Flexible

Finally, both parties must keep in mind that even though they may lay out their strategy well in advance of the negotiation session, they should still remain flexible. Unanticipated developments are very common in the course of the session. The negotiator must be alert, recognize these situations, and adjust his strategy accordingly in order to achieve his objectives.

The contractor should note that Federal Acquisition Regulation 15.807 requires the government to develop clear negotiation objectives prior to any pricing action.

Negotiation Conference

The agenda of the negotiation conference should be considered in advance of the session. The first order of business should be the normal "housekeeping" issues, such as drawing up a list of the individuals present and their positions in the respective organizations, as well as a statement of "the ground rules" and accepted procedures that the session will follow. Both parties should be certain, at the beginning of the session, that the representatives present have the authority to bind their respective organizations to any agreement that is reached. It can be very distressing to find out at the end of a negotiation session, when an apparent agreement has been reached, that the individual present must now go to some higher authority for approval.

Both parties should be punctual and should strive to maintain a cordial atmosphere and a calm and tolerant approach. Both sides should present their information in a clear and concise manner and, if at all possible, support their position with the appropriate documentation.

Generally, the first issue to be determined is the contractor's position on the matter at hand. The contractor should be prepared to state his position in concise, but complete, terms. The government, in turn, must be prepared to ask as many questions as necessary to obtain a clear definition of the contractor's position.

Once the contractor's position is clearly understood, it is up to the government representative to respond. At this stage, the government should be prepared to express its position or initiate its first counter-offer. The counter-offer should address all relevant issues presented by the contractor. Generally, the counter-offer will be the lowest possible offer that can be put on the table. At this point, both parties should understand one another's positions, and discussion can ensue regarding the various aspects of the two positions. When it becomes apparent that agreement cannot be reached on a particular aspect, both parties should strive to come up with an alternative in order to resolve the impasse.

During the negotiations, the objectives should be reiterated and the focus kept on the contractor's position. It is best not to stray into other areas of discussion. The negotiations may become clouded if the government cites safety or labor violations, nonconforming work, delays caused by the contractor or subcontractors, and/or unreasonable prices, in order to reduce the dollar amount. The prudent contractor must be aware of these tactics and be ready to counter them with facts.

Records of Negotiation

The Government
The government is required to record each negotiation session that occurs. This is true whether the meeting is to negotiate for

the contract itself or modifications/change orders to the contract. Federal Acquisition Regulation 15.808 requires this documentation, as it will become the official record and must be included in the contract files. This record becomes a part of the government's formal request to any higher authority for approval of either a prime contract or a contract modification.

The record of negotiation will include a reference to pricing data, and whether or not it is required in accordance with the Federal Acquisition Regulation. If cost data is not required, there should be a statement explaining the basis for the determination of price. The record should also indicate the degree to which the contractor's cost and pricing information is used. The basis for cost information is particularly important. If an audit is conducted at a future date and reveals that the cost information provided by the contractor was defective, the government must be able to show that it relied on that information in order to recover costs under the Truth in Negotiations Law. The record will also include information on how the government estimate was reached and how it was used during negotiations. It will further identify whether a government audit was used and to what degree it was relied on during the course of negotiations.

The Contractor
At the conclusion of the negotiations, the contractor should also make a written memo of the points of settlement. A joint written agreement may be made with the government, and its documents may be reviewed and approved by the contractor.

The Art of Negotiation

Everyone who has been involved in construction contracting has also been involved in some kind of negotiation. Everyone has his own particular negotiation techniques or "tricks of the trade." Rather than present a litany of possible techniques that can be used, the following items are intended to point out considerations that occur most often in government construction contracting.

Team Approach
In conducting negotiations, the government often uses a team approach. The "team" consists of the technical people involved in any issues concerning design or contract documents, the contract management or procurement people who are involved in the actual mechanics of modifying the contract, and the construction people who are involved in the actual day-to-day observation at the site. Normally, the contractor will find that the government representatives at the negotiation session far outnumber his own representatives. Heavy government representation should not intimidate the contractor. However, the contractor should, in turn, be prepared to bring with him key personnel capable of responding to the various issues that may arise during the negotiation session. When a team approach is used by either side, each team should thoroughly discuss the specific issues and which team member will address each issue prior to the negotiation session.

Use of Audits

Prior to a negotiation conference, the government will often perform an audit concerning a potential contract modification or negotiated prime contract. This information will not be released to the contractor, but rather will be used as a negotiating tool during the session. During negotiations, government representatives may take the position that the contractor's cost and pricing cannot be supported based on the results of the audit. At the same time, however, the government may refuse to share the results of the audit with the contractor. This is an unreasonable position for the government to take. For one thing, once the audit has been released by the audit agency, it becomes public information. At this point, the contractor has the right to obtain a copy. Furthermore, it is counterproductive to the negotiations if only one side has the audit information. It is in the best interest of both the government and the contractor for both to have ample opportunity to review the audit information prior to sitting down for negotiations.

Controlling the Session

Both parties should be interested in controlling the course of the discussion at the negotiation session. Both should prepare an agenda prior to the session so that the issues can be addressed in the proper sequence. It is generally in the best interest of both the government and the contractor to follow certain guidelines when drafting the negotiation agenda.

Change Orders

If the government and the contractor are negotiating a contract change order that involves both cost and time, the following issues should be considered:

1. First, does the situation reflect a true change? Does the required work differ from that spelled out in the contract requirements?
2. Once it has been agreed that a change exists, then the next question is, who is responsible for the change or where does the liability lie?
3. The next question addresses the impact of the change. Its effects may take many forms, such as extra work, overtime, loss of efficiency, and delays.
4. Once the effects have been defined, the overall price for the change can be estimated.

These four points should be addressed without fail. To depart from this four-step sequence allows one side or the other to resort to "circular arguments." Circular arguments may occur when two parties are discussing the price of a change. In one case, the government may not feel that the negotiated price is reasonable. The government representative may then say, "We don't believe we caused the change in the first place," which moves the entire discussion back to point two, after starting at point four. Proceeding chronologically from steps one through four, and solving each point in sequence, prevents either party from going back and raising questions regarding preceding issues.

"Rules"

Before a team from any organization enters into a negotiation session, it should have spelled out in advance a clear set of rules and guidelines. One principal negotiator should be designated by each negotiation team as the primary spokesperson for the group. Ahead of time, each team player should know what his role is and to what questions and issues he should be responding. Generally, his response will be at the direction of the team leader. While it is permissible for team members to offer comment during the course of the negotiation session, it is generally far more effective for each member to first be recognized by the team leader before participating in discussions.

Government Tactics

There are a number of games some negotiators play such as "good guy-bad guy," lack of funding to pay a higher settlement, lack of authority when the Contracting Officer later rejects the settlement, and the threat of an audit. The contractor may have already experienced some of these tactics. The best counteraction is to recognize it as a "game" and maintain a strong position on your objectives. Again, the key to a good negotiation and settlement is preparation. The government cannot sustain any "bluff" if the contractor is prepared with documented facts and reasons for the requested compensation.

The Rewards of Persistence

Negotiations can often be time-consuming and frustrating. Many times contractors dealing with the federal government lose patience and are inclined to walk away from the negotiation table and pursue legal remedies available through the contract. It is, however, in the contractor's best interest to pursue the negotiation route as aggressively as possible. Although it may appear that a contractor is not getting anywhere in resolving the problem, he should never give up. Government representatives may, in fact, understand and agree with many of the positions the contractor has taken, but for various reasons, may not be able to express this opinion during the sessions. After months of negotiation sessions, during which it appears that no headway has been made, the contractor may be surprised to discover in the very next session that the entire issue is resolved. The authors have seen this series of events on numerous occasions in negotiations with various government agencies.

Summary

Negotiation is such an important element of construction contracting that not only are there courses which explain negotiating techniques, but one government agency, the Corps of Engineers, publishes a book entitled *Construction Contract Negotiating Guide*. The Corps' guide covers contracts, contract modifications and the settlement of disputes. The guide offers a number of practical tips on negotiating, and defines the roles of the various government personnel involved in the negotiations.

The most important principle of negotiation is *preparation*. You cannot have a successful negotiating session without preparation. The contractor must gather the supporting facts and documents, define objectives, and select the persons who should attend the negotiation.

A solid command of the facts, with supporting documentation, enables the contractor to negotiate from a position of strength. The government negotiators will always seek a factual justification for any settlement because the record must reflect a legitimate basis for settlement and payment.

If negotiations prove unsuccessful, the contractor may have to file a claim with the government. Disputes with the federal government are described in general in Chapter 10, and the disputes procedure is detailed in Chapter 11.

Chapter Ten
Disputes with the Federal Government

Chapter Ten

Disputes with the Federal Government

Problems often arise during the course of a construction project which cannot be resolved in negotiations between the government and the contractor. The result is a *dispute*. When a situation reaches this level, the contractor must submit a claim on the dispute, and the government's Contracting Officer in charge of the project must issue a decision. An adverse decision may be appealed to either the appropriate agency Board of Contract Appeals or the United States Claims Court. Figure 10.1 is a general overview of the disputes procedure. This chapter contains descriptions of typical disputes. Guidelines are also provided for collecting information from the government — both about the project at hand and about past decisions. Instructions are also given for presenting the dispute to the government. The specific steps of the disputes procedure are explained in Chapter 11.

Evaluating Disputes

In order for the Contracting Officer to issue a decision on a dispute, or for a board or a court to reach a reasonable decision, both parties must prepare and present the facts as clearly as possible. This presentation is extremely important to the resolution of the dispute. Both the government and the contractor should first compile all facts to gain a thorough understanding of the issues. This means organizing all relevant documentation. The collected information should be thoroughly reviewed by both parties to evaluate the claim and to determine whether or not the contractor's claim is warranted. Disputes involve two major concerns. The first is the question of *entitlement*. The second is *cost*, or quantum.

Entitlement
When a contractor is seeking compensation for a change, the government and the contractor may disagree as to whether the change actually occurred. The government may assert that the contractor is not entitled to additional cost because nothing different was required from that which the contract originally specified.

An entitlement question may also arise over whether or not the contractor suffered any adverse impacts due to a change covered by the government. In this case, the government's position may be that while a change was made, it caused no extra work, delay, or impact to the contractor and, therefore, compensation is not justified.

Cost

A dispute may also arise if the contractor and the government cannot agree on the cost of a change. Some disputes involve both entitlement and quantum (cost), because the government

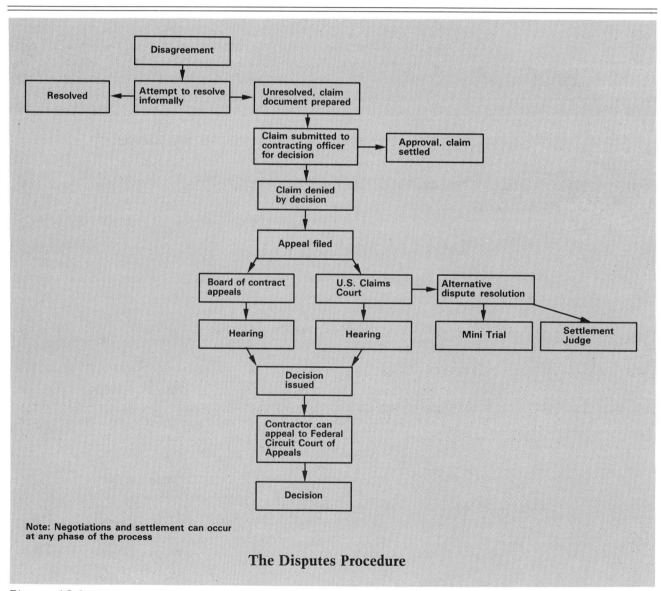

Note: Negotiations and settlement can occur at any phase of the process

The Disputes Procedure

Figure 10.1

and the contractor cannot agree on the impacts and damages resulting from an alleged change.

The Freedom of Information Act

In the early stages of a dispute, the contractor can request information concerning a particular project (and others like it) from the government under the *Freedom of Information Act* (FOIA). A Freedom of Information Act request is a simple procedure to initiate. The contractor merely writes a letter to the Freedom of Information Officer of the agency for whom he is working and requests the specified documents, or class of documents. The contractor should be sure that this request is not overly broad, since the government may take the position that too broad a request cannot reasonably be fulfilled. Likewise, the request should not be too specific, since the contractor may not pick up all the related information which would help to clearly assess the chances of winning the dispute.

The government must respond to a Freedom of Information Act request within ten days of when the request is made. The government will then produce the documents or may, upon request, allow the contractor to inspect and copy the documents at the government offices. This latter procedure is actually more advantageous to the contractor, because he can select the most pertinent documents.

What to Request

The Freedom of Information Act request is a very powerful tool which can assist both parties in resolving the dispute more rapidly. The types of documents that the contractor should request include:

- the government estimate for the project
- government estimates for any change orders that have been resolved
- government files, such as daily reports or quality control and quality assurance reports
- government files from the construction group, the procurement group, the finance and accounting group, and the design group, including correspondence with an outside architect/engineering firm

The contractor should not restrict itself to merely asking for a limited number of documents. Information that might greatly enhance the contractor's presentation may be contained in other files.

It is to the contractor's advantage to know how the government agencies set up their files. If the contractor is not well acquainted with government procedures, he should obtain the services of an outside counsel or consultant who is familiar with how the government sets up its documentation. By knowing what is available, the contractor can make a more thorough request under the Freedom of Information Act.

At this point, the government does not have an equal right to obtain information from the contractor. The government cannot request the contractor's documents until the dispute has moved into the *litigation* stage. In litigation, the government may acquire documents through *discovery* (the procedure in litigation where each party may examine the records and witnesses of the other side). The Freedom of Information Act may seem to be slanted toward the contractor, by granting him the greater access to documents. However, this arrangement is not necessarily harmful to the government. In reality, the more information the contractor has, the better able he is to substantiate and present his position and facilitate the ultimate resolution of the problem.

Charges for Documents

Regulations concerning the Freedom of Information Act requests have changed recently. If the contractor makes a request that would cost the government more than fifteen dollars, the government must inform the contractor of this charge in a written letter. Before the information is released, an agreement must be reached concerning payment to the government. The government usually presents an estimate of the cost and requests that the contractor pay this amount prior to the release of the documents.

When documents are requested for commercial use, a processing fee is charged for the costs of search, duplication, and review. These costs include expenses incurred during the initial examination of a document to determine if it is subject to exemption.

Documents Not Subject to Release

In certain cases, some of the documents requested are not subject to release under the Freedom of Information Act request. Among these cases are confidential documents involving internal correspondence, including correspondence with agency attorneys. If the government does not provide some documents because it believes they are not covered by the Freedom of Information Act, it must identify those documents that have been withheld. If the government does not adequately describe the documents, the contractor may request a more specific detailed description of the withheld documents, as well as the reasons they were not provided. (See Figure 2.4, Chapter 2, for a list of statutory exemptions to the FOIA.)

Legal Consultation

Once the contractor has acquired all necessary documents, he should update his files and study the facts carefully. He must develop a complete understanding of the issues involved, and prepare a very clear statement of his position regarding the dispute or claim.

In preparing his position, the contractor is well advised to consult qualified counsel. The term *qualified* is important. Qualified counsel means an attorney who has worked in the area of construction litigation and construction disputes. Preferably, the attorney consulted will have had prior experience with the federal government and, in particular, with disputes involving the federal government.

At this stage, a contractor should (through counsel) conduct some legal research to discover the precedents of the boards and the Claims Court. The purpose of this analysis is to determine how they have ruled on similar disputes. Without this knowledge, the contractor could waste a great deal of time and effort pursuing an issue that has been previously denied by the boards or court.

Reviewing prior decisions may also point out ways in which the contractor can substantiate a request for additional money or time. Presenting prior favorable court and board decisions can strengthen the contractor's position. Illustrations of such precedents can be very persuasive in convincing the government that the contractor's claims are legitimate.

The Claim Presentation

If informal discussions or negotiations regarding a claim prove fruitless, a clear, persuasive written claim must be prepared. There is no established format for the submission of a claim. However, a letter or report containing the following items is recommended.

- a statement of the pertinent facts
- reference to applicable specification provisions and contract clauses
- a factual/legal analysis

The letter or report that is submitted should refer all important documents, attaching each to the report as an exhibit. In this way, the reader will be able to review all of the pertinent data at one time.

The claim package is extremely important and should be prepared with care. This document is the basis for all reviews that may follow, including those before the Board of Contract Appeals or the United States Claims Court. It is essential, therefore, that the claim be well thought out and that the contractor develop one or more theories to substantiate the claim and the recovery. These theories should be supported by evidence, in both documentary and testimonial form.

The following points should be kept in mind during claim preparation:

- It is helpful to review prior Board of Contract Appeals and judicial decisions which involve similar factual and legal issues. Such a review may uncover supporting precedents or obstacles which must be overcome.
- Evidence should be gathered which will be useful in the event that legal proceedings are ultimately necessary.
- The Freedom of Information Act should be used to obtain documents from the government's files. Such documents may be included as part of the claim.
- The government's likely defenses to a claim should be anticipated and addressed in the submission.
- The need for legal and technical assistance should be evaluated in the preparation of a claim.

The Contract Disputes Act
The most important law with regard to the submission of claims and the disputes process is the *Contract Disputes Act of 1978* [41 U.S.C. 601-613]. The Act is incorporated into the disputes

clause of federal construction contracts [See FAR 52.233-1.], and it establishes the rights and obligations of the parties in pursuing disputes.

Certification

Claims over $50,000 must be certified in order to be valid. A certification such as that shown in Figure 10.2 should be included with the claim.

Certification is not necessary for claims under $50,000. Interest begins to accrue on a properly certified claim over $50,000, or an uncertified claim under $50,000, from the date of submission of the claim. The contractor's failure to certify, where required, will relieve the government from the responsibility to pay interest, and also will render a decision by the Contracting Officer unnecessary. Even if the Contracting Officer erroneously issues a decision on an uncertified claim (over $50,000), it has been held that the Board of Contract Appeals and United States Claims Court need not consider the appeal if the claim should have been certified according to the regulations.

Amount of the Claim

A claim should be for a specific amount; it should not be indefinite or qualified in any way. If it is impossible to determine an exact amount, it should be made clear that the claim has been based on reasonable estimates, and that these estimates will be revised as historical data becomes available. Failure to indicate that a claim is based on an estimate, rather than historical cost data, could lead to the allegation that a false claim was submitted, thereby constituting an act of fraud.

Once the contractor has organized his documentation, studied the information, and received some feedback from knowledgeable counsel, he can begin preparing the presentation of his claim or dispute.

The Purpose

One purpose should be kept in mind in the contractor's preparation of any request for extra compensation: *the contractor must prove that a change occurred.* In other words, he must show that something was required by the government which was different than that which was originally specified in the contract. To substantiate a deviation from the contract, he must relate his claim and the specific issues back to the contract. In whatever form the presentation is made, the contractor must relate the specific issues back to specific contract requirements. He must show that what was required by the government during the course of the project was indeed different from that which was specified originally in the contract documents. Remember, this presentation is, in a sense, a "sales pitch," intended to persuade the other side that the position is valid, and that the compensation is reasonable.

Organization of the Claim

There is no one best way to present a request for compensation to the government. There are numerous approaches which can be used. One general approach that the authors have found

CERTIFICATION OF A CLAIM

This is to certify that the foregoing claim is made in good faith; that the supporting data are accurate and complete to the best of my knowledge and belief; and that the amount requested accurately reflects the contract adjustment for which (Name of Company) believes the Government is liable.

NAME OF COMPANY

Date: _____   By: _____
                                       Name
                                       Title (Officer)

Figure 10.2

extremely successful in presenting claims to the federal government is discussed in the following section.

A claim document, or a document which would present the facets of a dispute, could be organized with the following parts:

1. Introduction
2. Project Execution/Project History
3. Liability and Impacts
4. Damages
5. Summary and Conclusions

Introduction

In the Introduction, the contractor should briefly describe the project and cite some of the problems which arose. The introduction should be limited to four or five pages, with the intent of acquainting an individual who may not be familiar with the project with items involved and the general nature of the project.

Project History

The second section, Project History, should be a narrative of the project execution. This section should chronologically examine what occurred during the project, concentrating on the salient facts. The Project History should start at the beginning of the job, listing the bid date and the number of bids received by the government, and proceed in the same fashion through the entire project. This portion of the presentation does not necessarily present every single detail, but should focus on those areas where changes, or the issues in the claim, have arisen.

Anything of particular significance should be supported with appropriate documentation. For example, if a statement is made that the government took a certain course of action on a specific date and there is a document to illustrate this action, then this document should be included as an exhibit to the report or presentation. Generally, it is a tremendous imposition to ask that the government go back and ferret out the same documentation. Since the contractor has already performed this research while preparing its claim, a copy of the document should be presented with the claim.

When writing the description of what occurred on a project, the contractor should make the statement as objective as possible, and avoid using terms that convey an opinion. A contractor should avoid using language such as that which appears in the following statement.

> "The shop drawings for the reinforcing bars for the foundation were submitted on the 3rd of January, 1987.[22] The contract absolutely required that the shop drawings be returned within 30 days.[23] The Government, in complete disregard of the contract, deliberately withheld the return of the shop drawings until the 30th of June,[24] thereby, intentionally delaying the contractor for over six months in the effective and efficient prosecution of the work and actually delaying the overall completion of job."

It is far more effective to present a strictly factual appeal. The same situation should, more appropriately, be worded as shown below:

> "The shop drawings for the reinforcing steel for the foundations were submitted on the 3rd of January, 1987.[22] The contract requires in Article 23.1 that the shop drawings would be reviewed and returned within 30 calendar days by the Government.[23] The shop drawings were returned by the Government on the 30th of June, 1987."[24]

The entire presentation should be presented in this manner. The superscripts, 22, 23, 24, refer to exhibits which substantiate the facts.

Whether a position is prepared by the government or the contractor, another point should be kept in mind. During the course of the analysis, the drafter should recognize that the entity he represents could have caused certain problems. This information should be included in the presentation of the facts. It will not help resolve the situation if either the contractor or the government ignores the fact that they may have delayed the project, caused the problem, or generated extra work. It is better to address one's responsibility, thereby helping to resolve the overall dispute more expeditiously. Sooner or later, the opposing side will raise adverse facts anyway and it reduces credibility if these facts have been omitted from the presentation.

Liability and Impacts

The third section, Liability and Impacts, should define the specific changes that occurred, identify who initiated the changes, and describe the impacts of those changes. The impacts may include effects such as extra work, inefficiency, delays, or idle equipment. It is here that the main issues of the dispute should be summarized and the impacts to either the contractor or the government described. A persuasive narrative in this section of the presentation will facilitate the acceptance of costs listed in the fourth section, Damages.

Damages

In the Damages section, the costs associated with the various impacts are listed. Completing this section should be relatively straightforward, if the impacts have been clearly defined. For instance, if a contractor had to work five extra hours with a crew of three men and a crane with one operator for a particular item of extra work, the cost of this activity is the cost to employ this crew, the equipment, and any material used.

The contractor should keep in mind that the costs presented in the damages section must be supportable. It is entirely possible that these costs will be audited; therefore, the contractor should be prepared to substantiate them with appropriate documentation. (Audits are discussed in Chapter 8.)

It is not necessary in the initial presentation to provide all backup documentation; this is normally an accounting task. The damages are generally presented according to the impacts that have been defined. Then the government is given the opportunity to verify the damages, if necessary.

Summary and Conclusions
The last section of the report is the Summary and Conclusions. This section is a summary of the facts and conclusions reached, including the "bottom line" position of the party presenting it.

Authority

The disputes procedure places the Contracting Officer in a very important role. He is the administrator of the contract for the government, and a decision maker whose responsibility is to step back and review disputes between the government staff and the contractor. Most importantly, the Contracting Officer has the authority to settle, compromise, pay, or otherwise adjust all claims by either party relating to the contract.

All claims are first submitted to the Contracting Officer for consideration and decision. Although the Contract Disputes Act does not, in itself, define a claim, regulations have defined a claim as a "written demand by one of the contracting parties seeking, as a legal right, the payment of money, adjustment or interpretation of contract terms or other relief, arising under or related to the contract." A claim must be submitted to the Contracting Officer before it can be reviewed by either the Board of Contract Appeals or the United States Claims Court.

Summary

The form of presentation outlined in this chapter has proven extremely effective and can be used by either the contractor or the government. In fact, if no resolution of the dispute is reached early on, this type of presentation should be used by both sides because it lays out all of the salient facts and backup information for the contracting officer or authority who might be making the final decision. Information collected for such a presentation will also serve as the basis for both the contractor's and government's cases should the disputes procedure be necessary.

Chapter Eleven
The Disputes Procedure

Chapter Eleven
The Disputes Procedure

The disputes procedure in federal government contracting is undoubtedly the fairest system available to construction contractors. The system provides a remedy for disputes and assures the contractor that his claim will be given impartial consideration. If disagreements as to additional costs or time cannot be settled amicably, this formal procedure guarantees third party administrative or judicial review. For reference, we have again shown the overview of the disputes procedure in Figure 11.1.

Despite the fairness and other merits of the federal disputes procedure, contractors should not initiate it every time there is a disagreement with a government agency. Both parties should first explore the possibility of an amicable settlement. It is much faster and considerably less expensive to resolve disputes if it can be done without filing a formal claim. If government representatives are convinced of the merits of a claim, they will often recognize that it is in everyone's interest to resolve the matter promptly — before the positions of the parties polarize. (Refer to Chapter 9, "Negotiations," for practical advice on entering into negotiations with government agencies.)

This chapter explains the disputes procedure step by step. It describes how an appeal should be filed and how to prepare for trial, and presents alternate dispute procedures.

The Government Decision

Once a properly certified claim has been submitted to the Contracting Officer, Section 6(a) of the Disputes Act requires that a decision be issued *in writing* within 60 days if the claim is less than $50,000, or within a "reasonable time" if the claim is over $50,000. The Contracting Officer must advise the contractor, within 60 days, of the time when a decision on a claim over $50,000 will be issued.

The decision should contain the following:

1. A description of the claim and dispute.
2. A reference to pertinent contract provisions.
3. A statement of the factual areas of agreement and disagreement.

4. A statement of the Contracting Officer's decision with supporting rationale.
5. A notice of the appeal rights available to the contractor.

Unfortunately, some Contracting Officers may try to put off the issue by continually asking the contractor for additional information when, in fact, sufficient information has been presented on which to decide the claim. However, a Contracting Officer is not justified in delaying the issuance of a decision merely because the contractor's data is inadequate. If the Contracting Officer believes that the contractor has not submitted sufficient information on which to base a decision, he

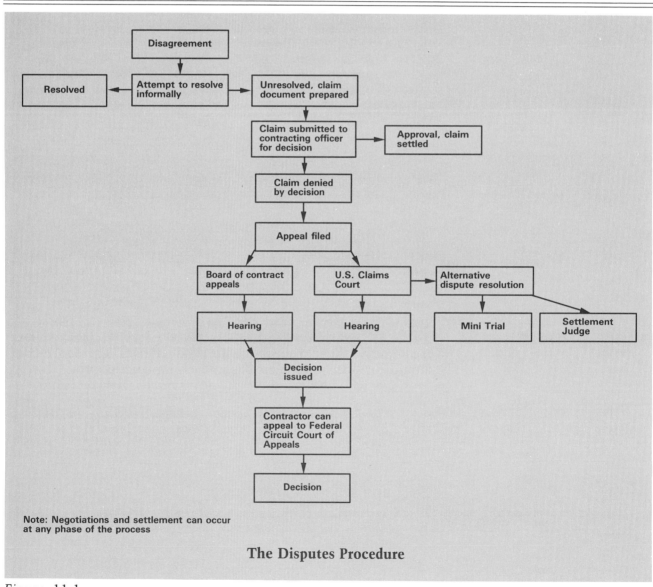

The Disputes Procedure

Figure 11.1

should give the contractor an opportunity to supplement the claim and, if additional information is not forthcoming, should issue a decision based on the information presented. The Contracting Officer cannot refuse to issue a decision on a properly certified claim.

Negotiations

The contractor should be aware that the opportunity to negotiate and resolve disputes does not cease merely because a formal claim has been submitted to the Contracting Officer. At all times, including the period during which the claim is under review by the Contracting Officer and even after a decision has been issued, the contractor should keep the dialogue open with government representatives and explore all possibilities of settlement. Government agencies are usually cooperative in such discussions and Contracting Officers are usually willing to meet and discuss differences of opinion.

Filing an Appeal

The Contracting Officer's decision may be to deny the contractor's claim — either totally or in substantial part. If the Contracting Officer fails to issue a written decision on a claim under $50,000 within 60 days, or within a "reasonable" time period for a claim over $50,000, this may be regarded as a "deemed denial" of the claim. The contractor has a right to treat the failure to issue a decision as though a decision had been issued denying the claim, and proceed according to the appeal rights described in the following section.

A Contracting Officer's decision, once issued, may be appealed *within 90 days* of receipt to the appropriate Board of Contract Appeals having jurisdiction over the contract, or within twelve months to the United States Claims Court. Once a contractor chooses to appeal to one of these forums, he may not later change his mind and go to the other legal entity. Filing a subsequent appeal in the other forum is generally regarded as "judge shopping" and is illegal. Therefore, it is very important that the contractor carefully weigh the decision as to whether to appeal to the Board of Contract Appeals or the Claims Court. There are no general rules to follow in making this decision, as the factors involved vary from case to case. For this reason, the decision should be discussed with legal counsel. The contractor should consider prior decisions in each jurisdiction, the attorneys who will represent the government (agency attorneys before the board, and the Justice Department before the Claims Court), and whether the claim is factually or legally complex.

Whether an appeal is directed to the Board of Appeals or to the U.S. Claims Court, the contractor must be aware that the failure to file within the required time periods will result in a loss of the right to appeal.

Board of Contract Appeals

An appeal may be taken to a Board of Contract Appeals by filing a *Notice of Appeal* within the required 90-day time period. This notice must be submitted in writing, signed by a person of authority (the contractor, an officer if the contractor is a corporation, or the contractor's attorney), and should identify the contract by number, the final decision which is being appealed, and the agency issuing the final decision. Although express mail services are sufficient if it is certain that the notice will be delivered prior to the expiration of the ninety days, it is safer to send the notice by registered mail. This provides irrefutable proof of mailing within the 90-day time period.

When a Notice of Appeal is filed with a Board of Contract Appeals, the government must prepare an administrative report, commonly referred to as the *Rule 4 File,* within 30 days. This file contains a copy of the Contracting Officer's decision, the claim, pertinent contract provisions, drawings, and correspondence which will assist the Board in reviewing the issues pertaining to the appeal. The contractor has the right to supplement the Rule 4 File; it is advisable that this be done at the earliest opportunity to ensure that the government has included all the necessary documents to permit a complete understanding of the case. At the trial, the Rule 4 File is customarily introduced into evidence and is available for both sides and their witnesses for ease of reference.

The contractor is also required, within 30 days of filing the Notice of Appeal, to file a *complaint* before the Board. This is a restatement of the claim and is a formal request for relief.

Although boards allow contractors to represent themselves, it is generally advisable to seek legal assistance. The government is always represented by legal counsel, and few contractors have the training and expertise to properly present the case for trial, or to argue legal issues. By the same token, many contractors are more capable of addressing technical issues than are their attorneys. Therefore, the technical expertise of the contractor and the legal expertise of the attorney should be combined to present the case in a clear and persuasive manner.

Government Answer

The government has 30 days following receipt of the contractor's complaint to file its answer. The answer responds to each and every allegation in the complaint and sets forth any affirmative defenses that the government may have. In this way, the parties are required to state their respective positions so that the board may identify and frame the issues which will later be heard at the trial.

Other Options

One advantage in proceeding with an appeal before the board, rather than the U.S. Claims Court, is that the contractor may request an *accelerated procedure* if the claim involves $50,000 or less. The optional accelerated procedure requires that a Board decision be issued within 180 days following the Notice of Appeal.

Similarly, if the appeal involves $10,000 or less, the contractor may elect the *expedited procedure* which provides for a Board decision within 120 days after filing the Notice of Appeal.

U.S. Claims Court

If the contractor elects to proceed before the United States Claims Court, a complaint must be filed with the Court within

12 months of receipt of the Contracting Officer's decision. Corporations or contractors *must* be represented by an attorney. It is therefore important to allow counsel sufficient time to prepare the papers necessary to start an action in the United States Claims Court. The Claims Court practice is similar to that of the Board of Contract Appeals in that after the contractor has filed his initial complaint, the government files its answer. Although the government is usually represented by the agency's counsel in a matter before a Board of Contract Appeals, the Justice Department typically provides representation on matters that go to the United States Claims Court. The pre-trial procedures that follow the filing of the complaint and answer are virtually the same in both Board and Court practice.

Preparing the Case

In order to prepare adequately for trial, it is important for the contractor to engage in *discovery* of the opposition's case. Discovery is the process of obtaining evidence from the other party, information intended to support one's case, to provide background on the other party's case. Discovery typically takes the following forms:

- **Interrogatories:** Written questions about pertinent and relevant matters which the other side must answer within 30 days.
- **Production of Documents:** A request for the right to review and copy the other party's documents that pertain to the case.
- **Depositions:** Interviews of the other party's witnesses before a court reporter to determine what they know about the case, and what they are prepared to testify about should the case go to trial.
- **Requests for Admissions:** Written statements submitted to the other side which, unless objected to, will admit pertinent facts.

Expert Witnesses

Judges often need assistance in deciding technical matters. One way to obtain this assistance is through the use of an expert witness. This individual should have sufficient experience and educational background to be considered an expert witness. The witness should also be articulate and capable of testifying in a persuasive manner, and should be an individual who can "think on his feet."

It is helpful to obtain the services of an expert witness early in the case. If possible, allow the expert witness to become involved, visiting the site, for example, while the project is underway, and later testifying as to his observations. A properly prepared and qualified expert can often make a favorable impression on the judge and will help support the case.

Negotiation

Filing a claim does not mean that the dispute cannot be negotiated and settled. In fact, a significant number of disputes and claims are settled before going to the Board of Contract Appeals or U.S. Claim Court. Negotiation and settlement may occur at any time during the disputes process. See Chapter 9, for more detailed information on negotiations.

Settlement

If the dispute is settled prior to a hearing, the government issues a *bilateral contract modification* (both parties must sign) on the terms and dollar amount agreed to. The contractor should also agree to a date by which it is to receive this contract modification. Payment is either concurrent with the modification or, as normally occurs, subsequent to the execution and return of the modification to the government. If the dispute has been brought before a Board of Contract Appeals, the case should also be formally dismissed. This dismissal is subject to reinstatement should the government fail to pay the settlement amount.

The Trial

If pre-trial settlement discussions and negotiations fail to resolve the dispute, the trial will take place at the appointed time. Whether the trial is before a Board of Contract Appeals or the United States Claims Court, it involves a hearing before a judge. The hearing is more formal if it takes place in the United States Claims Court.

The contractor has the burden of proof and, therefore, is required to present its case first. Each witness and exhibit presented to support the claim should have a particular purpose and should support the basic theory of the case. It is important to remember that the judge is not as familiar with the facts as are the two parties. The issues should be presented in a manner which is both understandable and persuasive.

Each side will have the opportunity to cross-examine the witnesses of the other side. A transcript will be kept by a court reporter. The judge may have questions of the witnesses in addition to those asked by the attorneys; each side should be prepared to address any questions raised by the judge.

Cases that go to trial are usually *bifurcated* or divided into two parts. These parts are *entitlement* and *quantum*. As explained in Chapter 10, entitlement deals with whether or not there is merit in the contractor's position, and quantum concerns the amount to which the contractor is ultimately entitled. Since judges do not like to waste time hearing testimony about how much money was lost unless it has already been determined that the contractor is entitled to compensation, the boards and court will usually bifurcate the case and try entitlement only. This means that the trial will focus on the issue of whether and why the contractor is entitled to compensation, and the decision will address these issues only.

If the contractor wins an entitlement decision, the matter is then *remanded*, or passed back to the Contracting Officer for negotiation and payment. If, however, the parties cannot agree on quantum, or cost, then the matter is again brought to the judge for a decision on this question. A favorable decision on entitlement usually assures the contractors of a satisfactory resolution of quantum as well.

Alternate Dispute Resolution

Contractors should be aware that formal trials are no longer the only litigation choice. In response to rising litigation costs and the delay often inherent in the traditional judicial resolution of complex legal claims, the United States Claims Court recently implemented two methods of *alternative dispute resolution* (ADR) to help contractors resolve disputes more expeditiously. As a result, contractors who appeal to the U.S. Claims Court now have the option of presenting their case to a *Settlement Judge* or pursuing a *Mini-Trial* in an attempt to promote an early settlement of their claim. In addition, contractors are encouraged to adopt other ADR techniques which do not require court involvement, such as arbitration by experts.

Whether these ADR techniques can save time and money depends on the specific facts of the case. The ADR procedures administered by the Court are voluntary, and should be employed early in the litigation process to minimize *discovery*, the pre-trial proceeding for identifying the key facts in the case. As these procedures involve the application of judicial resources, the court believes their use is most appropriate where the parties anticipate a lengthy discovery period, followed by a long trial. These conditions are typically met when the amount in dispute exceeds $100,000 and the trial is expected to last more than one week.

Once the parties decide to pursue one of the ADR methods offered, the case is reassigned to a new judge who presides over the ADR proceedings. Should the technique adopted fail to produce a settlement, the case is returned to the original judge's docket and normal trial preparation continues. Because ADR proceedings are designed to promote settlement, all representations are confidential and may not be used for any reason in subsequent litigation.

The following brief description of the available ADR procedures should prove helpful in determining whether they are appropriate for a case.

Settlement Judge

With this alternative, the parties present their case to a neutral advisor who evaluates the strengths and weaknesses of the case. Flexible and informal, settlement judge proceedings last only a day or two and can be used successfully at any stage of the litigation. Because the case is returned to the original judge if settlement is not reached, the parties gain the benefit of a judicial assessment of their settlement positions without jeopardizing their ability to obtain an impartial decision in the traditional court system.

Mini-Trial

The mini-trial is an expedited procedure wherein each party presents an abbreviated version of the case to a neutral advisor. The advisor assists the parties in negotiating a settlement. Mini-trials are best suited for settling fact-intensive cases which do not present novel issues of law or depend on witness credibility. The following guidelines will govern most mini-trial proceedings.

Time Frame

The entire process, including discovery and trial, should conclude within one to three months.

Participants

Senior management and agency officials with first-hand knowledge of the case should participate in the mini-trial. Both sides may have legal representation.

Discovery

Discovery should be limited in scope and scheduled to conclude two weeks prior to the mini-trial. Any discovery disputes which the parties cannot resolve are handled by the mini-trial judge. Discovery taken for mini-trial may be used in further judicial proceedings if settlement is not reached.

Pre-Hearing Matters

After discovery, the parties meet with the mini-trial judge and present brief written summaries of their respective positions. Stipulations for the hearing are finalized, and witness lists and exhibits are exchanged.

Hearing

The hearing is informal and generally should not exceed one day. The rules of evidence and procedure will not apply and the parties may structure their case to include examination of witnesses, the use of demonstrative evidence, and oral argument. The judge's role is flexible and may include questioning of witnesses.

Post-Hearing Settlement Discussions

After the hearing, the parties and counsel meet to discuss resolution of the dispute. The judge may participate in the discussion or offer an advisory opinion concerning the merits of the claim. If settlement is not reached, the case returns to the original judge.

A Final Word on ADR

ADR represents the court's attempt to resolve disputes before contractors and government agencies invest a considerable amount of time and money in contesting the matter. As such, the mini-trial and Settlement Judge hearings offer an important alternative to traditional court procedures. Federal agencies, most notably the Army Corps of Engineers, have also initiated their own form of mini-trial procedures which contractors should investigate and invoke whenever practical.

Summary

The federal disputes procedure provides for a fair and impartial review of Contracting Officer decisions, but it is not a substitute for the amicable resolution of problems through negotiation. In order for disputes to be resolved early, it is necessary for each side to be open-minded and prepared. It is, therefore, necessary for each side to do its "homework" and to participate in the "give and take" that occurs in any dispute resolution.

Construction contractors should do everything possible to avoid litigation by keeping the dialogue with agency representatives open, and by utilizing the alternate dispute resolution procedures outlined in this chapter. Those who litigate on "matters of principle" only should be prepared to incur substantial litigation costs. It is preferable to establish specific, realistic objectives before engaging in litigation, and to encourage a compromise which saves the time and effort of formal litigation. If a trial is necessary, however, those who are the best prepared will invariably be the most likely to prevail.

Chapter Twelve
Differences Among the Federal Agencies

Chapter Twelve
Differences Among the Federal Agencies

Government agencies often issue their own regulations in addition to those set by the Federal Acquisition Regulation. Consequently, the conduct and administration of a construction project may vary from one agency to another. This chapter addresses some of the most significant regulations encountered when working with government agencies.

Agency Construction Policies

U.S. Postal Service
The U.S. Postal Service is an independent agency of the federal government. It is, therefore, not bound by the Federal Acquisition Regulation. Rather, its procurements are governed by the U.S. Postal Service Procurement Manual (issued on October 1, 1987). This manual establishes Postal Service policy regarding the procurement of supplies, services, construction, and mail transportation, and incorporates many of the contract clauses contained in the Federal Acquisition Regulation.

The Veterans Administration
The Veterans Administration (VA) generally administers contracts by one of two methods. The first method involves the following procedures and assignment of responsibility. The VA executes and administers most major contracts from its Central Office in Washington, where the agency employs four *Contracting Officers* for the entire United States. The actual day-to-day work is supervised by a Contracting Officer's representative, the *Resident Engineer*, and his assistants, known as *Assistant Resident Engineers*. These representatives have specified levels of authority which allow them to direct changes up to certain dollar amounts. However, the contract is entered into by the Contracting Officer in Washington, D.C., who has the ultimate authority concerning contract decisions and changes.

The second method of administering VA contracts is by designating a contracting officer at the *installation level*. For example, an individual may be designated as the Contracting Officer at a VA Hospital where construction is required. Although this method has typically been used for small-scale projects, the Veterans Administration is in the process of decentralizing its contract administration function so that more of its larger-scale projects will be run in this manner.

Generally, the contracts administered from the Central Office (in Washington) are run by an experienced staff, which has worked on numerous construction projects throughout the country. The Contracting Officers assigned to projects performed at the installation level may not have the same level of experience as do the Contracting Officers from the Central Office. As a result, the Contracting Officer at the installation level may not be as familiar with the Federal Acquisition Regulation and other administrative procedures that the Veterans Administration follows.

U.S. Army Corps of Engineers

The Corps of Engineers normally runs its projects from District Offices. The Contracting Officer may be a District Engineer or, for smaller projects, a Deputy District Engineer. Normally, the District Engineer is either a Colonel or a Lieutenant Colonel, while the Deputy District Engineer may be a Colonel, a Lieutenant Colonel, or a Major. Contracts for large projects may be administered out of a Division Office. The Corps of Engineers Division Office is a level above the District Office and normally encompasses several districts. When contracts are administered by a Division Office, the Division Engineer (who may be a General) or the Deputy Division Engineer (who may be a Colonel or Lieutenant Colonel) might be the Contracting Officer.

Naval Facilities Engineering Command

The Navy runs its projects from two main headquarters. The Contracting Officers run the projects from one of these two sites. The actual physical administration of the project is run by an *Officer in Charge of Construction* (OICC) or a *Resident Officer in Charge of Construction* (ROICC) stationed at the site. Because of the central location of the Contracting Officers in the Navy (and the Veterans Administration Central Office projects), it is more difficult for the contractor to directly communicate with the Contracting Officer. The contractor must convey all communications through the designated government representative(s) on the site.

The Air Force

The Air Force administers its projects at the installation level. A Contracting Officer is designated for each project, to work at the installation level. The Contracting Officer may be either a civilian or an officer (ranging in rank from Lieutenant through General). Most major Air Force construction projects are managed by the Corps of Engineers, with the Air Force administering the smaller repair, maintenance, and construction contracts.

Schedules

The various agencies have different scheduling requirements. These requirements are described in the following paragraphs.

Veterans Administration

The Veterans Administration has an extremely specific scheduling requirement. The contractor must submit a Critical Path Method (CPM) schedule that is both resource- and cost-loaded.

Corps of Engineers

The Corps of Engineers may require schedules varying from a very simple bar chart to a very detailed CPM schedule. In the past, most Corps of Engineers' projects have required only a bar chart, but the items on the bar chart had to be cost-loaded. Based on the cost-loaded bar chart, the contractor draws an "S-Curve" demonstrating the dollars over time that the contractor will invoice in accordance with his schedule. Figure 12.1 is an example of this transfer of information.

When changes occur, the contractor is required to update costs on both the bar chart and the S-Curve. More and more Corps Districts now are requiring Critical Path Method schedules, similar to those that the Veterans Administration has required.

Other Agencies

Other agencies' scheduling requirements vary dramatically. For the most part, however, agencies require only a bar chart type of schedule, and, possibly, an S-Curve. In a few instances, a detailed Critical Path Method schedule may be required.

Changes

The various agencies also have different methods for administering contract changes. The particular change requirements for each agency are described in the following paragraphs.

Corps of Engineers

The United States Army Corps of Engineers executes changes through a mechanism known as a *change order*. The Corps does not have any other mechanism for making changes. However if, for some reason, a change order cannot be processed or the Corps is not able to come to terms with the contractor, it will issue a written directive to perform the work and later resolve it as a contract modification.

Veterans Administration

By contrast, the Veterans Administration uses *formal change orders*, *field proceed orders*, and *central office proceed orders*. A proceed order is used when time does not allow for the formal execution of a change order. Field proceed orders are issued by the Resident Engineer in the field. However, the field proceed order can only be issued for changes within the limits of authority of the Resident Engineer. If the amount of work that must be performed exceeds the Resident Engineer's limit of authority, then the Veterans Administration must be notified and must issue a central office proceed order, signed by the Contracting Officer.

For both field proceed orders and central office proceed orders, the Veterans Administration specifies a "not-to-exceed" price or maximum dollar limit. These are like change orders in that the contractor bills the agency and is paid for the work. However,

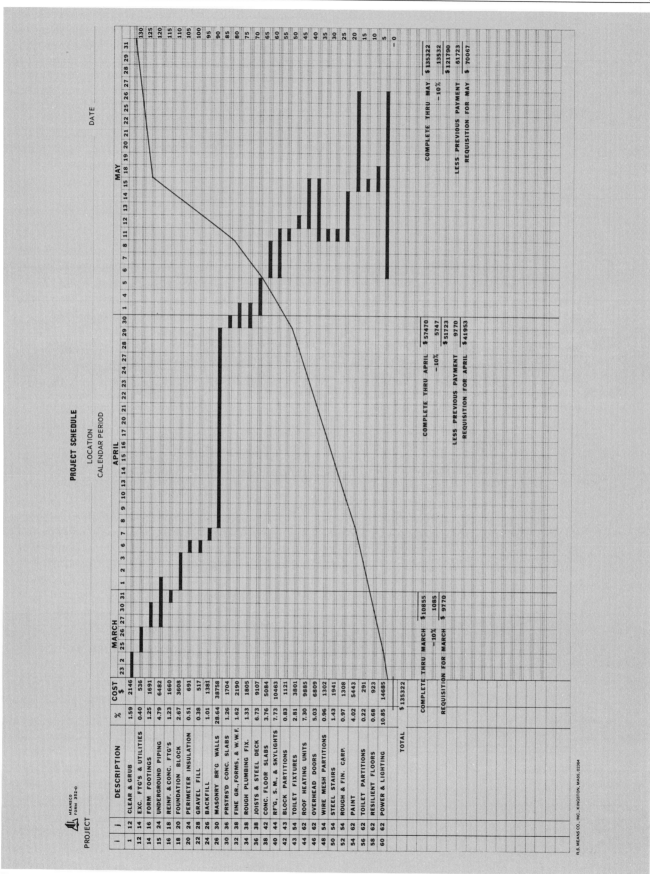

Figure 12.1

188

the contractor's invoice cannot exceed the amount specified on the change order. For example, the Veterans Administration may issue a field or central office proceed order for $5,000 to perform certain work. The contractor performing that work can then bill the agency up to that $5,000 amount.

Other agencies do not allow any form of billing until a *formal change order* is executed. Therefore, the Veterans Administration is generally more fair in paying contractors for extra work associated with changes to the contract.

Other Issues
In the course of administering change orders, there are some other differences from agency to agency. The Veterans Administration, for example, is the only agency that requires all of its change orders to be connected to a specific activity on the critical path method schedule. Few, if any, other agencies have this requirement. In the past, the Veterans Administration used a sliding scale with a percentage for overhead and a percentage for profit to be allowed on change orders. As the dollar value of the change order increased, the percentage mark-up allowed decreased. A recent General Accounting Office decision has invalidated this Veterans Administration Policy. Since such changes in policy often occur, the contractor should consult with legal counsel to determine the current applicability of such clauses.

Disputes

If a construction problem is handled through the channels of the disputes process, there are several forums (depending on the agency for which the contractor is working) before which the issue may be heard. A disputed Contracting Officer's decision may be appealed to different Boards of Contract Appeals. For example, a dispute with the Corps of Engineers on the construction of a civil works project (dam, dredging, riprap) will go to the *Corps of Engineers Board of Contract Appeals*, while the dispute with the United States Navy or Air Force may go to the *Armed Services Board of Contract Appeals*, and a dispute with the Veterans Administration may go to the *Veterans Administration Board of Contract Appeals*.

All appeals of a Contracting Officer's decision may be submitted to the United States Claims Court, no matter which agency issued the decision.

A Final Word on Government Contracting

The variety of procedures employed by the federal agencies who engage in construction contracting make it necessary for contractors to learn about each agency's organization and particular methods of contract administration. Nevertheless, despite the differences from agency to agency, there is a great deal of fairness and consistency in the federal acquisition system. The safeguards included in federal construction contracts provide administrative review at many levels, thereby ensuring an objective resolution of disputes.

Clearly those contractors who are able to complete their projects without claims, or with only a minimum number of disputes, are the most likely to be successful and profitable. None of the information in this book should serve to encourage contractors to utilize the disputes process as a way to overcome improvident bidding, or to attempt to obtain undeserved profits. The fact is, disputes consume the contractor's time and money, and the formal disputes process should only be employed when amicable means of resolving disputes have been exhausted.

The authors have endeavored to address the important issues and to suggest the most appropriate ways for contractors to protect their rights and to take full advantage of the protections afforded by the federal system. It is important, however, to do everything possible to keep abreast of recent developments by reading trade publications, books, and newsletters which focus on federal construction issues.

If a problem develops which cannot be addressed by the contractor, experts should be consulted at the earliest opportunity. Many problems can be minimized if they are addressed quickly and forcefully. Finally, in dealing with any federal agency, it is important to find out who has the decision-making authority and to attempt to meet with that individual as soon as possible. Objectivity often increases with high levels of responsibility and authority.

Abbreviations

AGBCA — Agricultural Board of Contract Appeals
ASBCA — Armed Services Board of Contract Appeals
CBD — Commerce Business Daily
CICA — Competition in Contracting Act
COC — Certificate of Competency
CPM — Critical Path Method
DAR — Defense Acquisition Regulation
DOD — Department of Defense
DOE — Department of Energy
DOT — Department of Transportation
EFAR — Engineer Federal Acquisition Regulation
FAR — Federal Acquisition Regulation
FOIA — Freedom of Information Act
FPR — Federal Procurement Regulation
GAO — Government Accounting Office
GSA — General Services Administration
GSBCA — General Services Board of Contract Appeals
NSA — Network Analysis System
NASA — National Aeronautic & Space Administration
OMB — Office of Management & Budget
QAE — Quality Assurance Engineers
SBA — Small Business Administration
SF — Standard Form
USC — United States Code
VA — Veterans Administration
VAAR — Veterans Administration Acquisition Regulation

Glossary of Terms

Abstract of Bids
A list of the bidders for a sealed bid procurement indicating the significant portions of their bids.

Acceleration
An ordered or voluntarily expedited performance necessary for recapturing project delay.

Acceptance
Compliance by an offeree with the terms and conditions of an offer.

Accord & Satisfaction
An agreement between parties to a contract whereby one accepts payment in the compromise of a dispute, claim, or change proposal (see Settlement).

Act of God
An act, event, or happening resulting from natural causes without interference or aid from man.

Administrative Remedy
A non-judicial remedy provided by an agency, board, commission, or the like.

Agency Law
Rules, regulations, and procedures promulgated by an agency.

Agent
Relation in which one person acts for or represents another.

Allocable Cost
A cost which is assignable to a particular contract or other cost objective.

Allowable Cost
Any reasonable cost which, according to the FAR, may be recovered under the contract to which it is allocable.

Appeal Notice

A notice to a Board of Contract Appeals that a Contracting Officer's final decision or failure to issue a decision will be appealed.

Arbitration

Reference of a dispute to an impartial third person chosen by the parties to the dispute, who agree in advance to abide by the arbitrator's decision after a hearing at which both parties have an opportunity to be heard.

Audit

The examination of records, documents, and other evidence for the purpose of determining the propriety of transactions and assessing the contractor's compliance with relevant cost and accounting requirements.

Bid Bond

A surety bond which protects the government in the event that the winning bidder fails to execute the contract documents and proceed with performance.

Bidders Mailing List

A list of contractors to whom the government sends invitations for bids for particular procurements.

Bid Guarantee

An instrument, including a bid bond, which protects the government in the event that the winning bidder fails to execute the contract documents and proceeds with performance.

Bid Protest

A challenge by a disappointed bidder usually submitted to the Contracting Officer or the GAO against the award of a government contract.

Bilateral Contract

A contract in which both contracting parties are bound to fulfill obligations reciprocally towards each other.

Brand Name or Equal

A type of product description which identifies one or more commercial products by brand name and which sets forth those characteristics of the named product essential to the government's needs.

Breach of Contract

Failure, without legal cause, to perform any promise under a contract.

Buy-In

A bidder's attempt to win a contract by submitting a price which will result in a loss, with the hope of making the contract profitable through change orders or follow-on contracts.

Cardinal Change

A contract change which alters the basic nature of the work the parties bargained for when the contract was awarded, thereby constituting a breach of contract by the government.

Change

Any action that causes a revision or addition to the contractor's original contract requirements.

Change Order

A written order pursuant to the Change Clause of the contract directing the contractor to make changes to the contract work.

Claim

A contractor's request for additional compensation or an extension of time pursuant to the contract terms.

Compensatory Damages

An award which compensates a party for actual injuries or damages sustained.

Constructive Acceleration

A requirement that a contractor complete his work earlier than the contract time, including time extensions to which he is entitled because of excusable delays.

Constructive Change

A change to a contract resulting from conduct by the government which has the effect of requiring the contractor to perform work different from that presented in the contract.

Contract

An agreement between two parties to perform work or provide goods, including an agreement or order for the procurement of supplies or services.

Contract Change

A change to the contract requirements within the general and contract clauses.

Contract Modification

Any unilateral or bilateral written alteration of the contract in accordance with the governing regulations and contract clauses.

Contract Type

Specific pricing arrangements are employed for the performance of work under contracts. These arrangements include firm fixed-price, fixed-price-incentive, cost-plus-fixed-fee, cost-plus-incentive-fee, and several others.

Contracting Officer

The representative of a government agency with authority to bind the government in contract matters.

Contracting Officer's Decision

The contracting Officer's final ruling regarding a properly submitted claim.

Cost-Reimbursement Contract

A type of contract in which the pricing arrangement involves the payment of allowable costs incurred by the contractor during performance.

Debarment

The formal sanction by the government prohibiting a contractor from receiving contracts as a result of certain proscribed actions including crimes, fraud, etc.

Deductive Change

A change resulting in a reduction in contract price.

Default

An omission or failure to perform a contractual duty.

Delay

An extension to the planned contract completion date or to elements of project operations caused by action or inaction by either the owner or the contractor.

Design Specification

A type of specification which prescribes the materials and methods to be used for contract performance.

Differing Site Conditions

Unanticipated physical conditions at the site which differ materially from those set forth in the contract or ordinarily encountered in work of the nature provided.

Discovery

A pretrial procedure providing for the full disclosure of all facts and documents related to a contract dispute.

Dispute Procedure

The administrative procedure for processing a dispute arising under a contract. This procedure is provided for in the contract by the Contract Disputes Act, applicable to contracts with the United States government.

Disruption

Disruption results from actions or inactions which interfere with performance efficiency requiring additional effort in performance of the contract work.

Equitable Adjustment

An adjustment to the contract price or time resulting from a change, differing site condition, or the like, which compensates the contractor for reasonable costs, plus overhead and profit.

Excess Reprocurement Costs

Additional costs which the government incurs following a default termination to reprocure the defaulted quantity of supplies, services, or unfinished work.

Excusable Delay
A delay to contract performance which is beyond control, fault, or negligence of the contractor. If a delay is determined to be excusable, the government cannot initiate a termination for default.

Extended Overhead
Overhead costs accumulated during compensable delay periods when full production was not achievable.

Fixed-Price Contract
A type of contract in which the contractor agrees to perform for an established price, agreed in advance.

Flow-Downs
Clauses from a prime contractor's contract with the government that are incorporated into the prime's subcontracts.

GAO
The U.S. General Accounting Office which, under the direction of the Comptroller General of the United States, has jurisdiction over bid protests. The GAO is an arm of the Congress.

Implied Contract
A contract not created by explicit agreement between the parties, but inferred by law from their acts or conduct.

Industry Specification
A type of specification prepared by technical or industry associations that is approved for use by federal agencies.

Interest Expense
A contractor's cost of borrowing funds or use of equity capital.

Invitation for Bids
Information forwarded to potential bidders requesting bids for a sealed bid procurement.

Jurisdiction
The authority of a judicial or administrative forum to hear and resolve disputes.

Liquidated Damages
A specific sum of money which has been expressly stipulated by the parties to a contract as the amount of damages to be recovered in the event of a breach.

Litigation
A lawsuit or other adversary proceeding to resolve disputes by conducting a hearing and presenting arguments to a judge for a decision.

Meeting of the Minds
A mutual agreement to the terms and conditions of a contract.

Mitigation of Damages
The duty to minimize damages following a breach of contract.

Negotiated Procurement
A procedure for contracting whereby the government and potential contractor negotiate on both price and technical requirements after submission of proposals. Award is made to the contractor whose final proposal is most advantageous to the government.

Notice to Proceed
A written order by the government to the contractor to proceed with the contract work.

Offer
A manifestation of willingness to enter into a contract.

Payment Bond
A bond which secures a contractor's obligation to properly complete the contract work.

Performance Bond
A bond which secures a contractor's obligation to properly complete the contract work.

Performance Specification
A type of specification which sets forth an end result, leaving the method of performance up to the contractor.

Privity of Contract
This occurs when a party has a direct contractual relationship with another party.

Progress Payment
A periodic contract payment made as work progresses.

Proposal
A submission by the contractor used as the basis for awarding or pricing a contract.

Reasonable Cost
A cost which would be incurred by an ordinarily prudent person in the conduct of competitive business.

Request for Proposals (RFP)
Material provided to potential contractors to communicate government requirements and solicit proposals.

Responsibility
A bidder's ability to properly perform the contract work.

Responsiveness
The bid's conformance with the solicitation's salient requirements (price, quantity, quality, performance time).

Sealed Bidding
A basic method of procurement which involves the solicitation of bids and the award of a contract to the responsible bidder submitting the lowest responsive bid.

Settlement
An agreement by which the parties consent to settling a dispute between them.

Specification
A detailed description of the contract performance requirements.

Statute of Limitations
A time limit established by statute within which one may file a notice of appeal or initiate a lawsuit.

Substantial Performance
Performance which deviates only in minor respects from the contract's requirements, thereby precluding a termination for default.

Supplemental Agreement
A change to an existing contract which is accomplished by the mutual action of the parties.

Suspension of Work
A situation where the contractor must stop performance of the contract work due to the action or inaction of the government.

Termination for Convenience
The unilateral right of the government to terminate contracts at will.

Termination for Default
A sanction which the government may impose for a contractor's unexcused failure to perform.

Two-Step Sealed Bidding
A procurement method whereby contractors submit technical proposals in response to government performance specifications. Each contractor whose technical proposal is acceptable then submits a sealed bid in accordance with normal bidding procedures.

Unilateral Modification
A change in the contract requirements unilaterally directed by the government.

Index